New Nutshells

Criminal Law

AUSTRALIA
The Law Book Company Ltd.
Sydney : Melbourne : Brisbane

CANADA AND U.S.A.
The Carswell Company Ltd.
Agincourt, Ontario

INDIA
N.M. Tripathi Private Ltd.
Bombay
and
Eastern Law House Private Ltd.
Calcutta
M.P.P. House
Bangalore

ISRAEL
Steimatzky's Agency Ltd.
Jerusalem : Tel Aviv : Haifa

MALAYSIA : SINGAPORE : BRUNEI
Malayan Law Journal (Pte.) Ltd.
Singapore

NEW ZEALAND
Sweet and Maxwell (N.Z.) Ltd.
Wellington

PAKISTAN
Pakistan Law House
Karachi

New Nutshells

Criminal Law

Steve Brandon

London
Sweet & Maxwell
1979

First Edition 1979
Second Impression 1981

Published by
Sweet & Maxwell Ltd. of
11 New Fetter Lane, London
Computerset by
MFK Graphic Systems (Typesetting) Ltd., Saffron Walden
Printed in Great Britain by
J. W. Arrowsmith Ltd., London and Bristol

ISBN 0 421 25610 9

Series Introduction

New Nutshells present the essential facts of law. Written in clear, uncomplicated language, they explain basic principles and highlight key cases and statutes.

New Nutshells meet a dual need for students of law or related disciplines. They provide a concise introduction to the central issues surrounding a subject, preparing the reader for detailed complementary textbooks. Then, they act as indispensable revision aids.

Produced in a convenient pocketbook format, *New Nutshells* serve both as invaluable guides to the most important questions of law and as reassuring props for the anxious examination candidate.

Criminal Law looks at procedure and the burden of proof before explaining the concepts of *actus reus, mens rea*, strict and vicarious liability. Subsequent chapters deal with accomplices, inchoate offences, homicide and assaults. There is a lengthy consideration of theft and the work concludes with a section on defences.

Contents

		page
Series Introduction		v
	Introduction	1
1	Preliminary Concepts	3
2	Accomplices	15
3	Inchoate Offences	20
4	Homicide	32
5	Offences against the Person Act 1861	46
6	The Theft Act (1)	52
7	The Theft Act (2)	68
8	The Theft Act (3)	79
9	Defences	85
Index		95

INTRODUCTION

This book is an aid to the passing of examinations in criminal law; it is not a textbook. No student will gain an understanding of the subject until he has read weightier tomes and, more importantly, the major cases, for in the end, the law can only be predicted by an understanding of why leading cases were decided as they were.

Concentration in this book will be on providing a framework, and on the problems which examiners tend to draw on, year in, year out. Always remember that the examiner wants to know that you understand the law; not merely that you can recite the names of legion of semi-relevant cases. Remember also that questions often involve consideration of more than one area of the criminal law—always look carefully to see how many separate points are involved. Always plan your answer carefully, listing each of these points in order and stick to that plan—this avoids repetition, the bane of an examiner's life. Stick to the point—examiners are not fooled by waffle, and remember that it is seldom necessary to recite the facts of manor cases in great detail—highlight facts only when directly relevant to your argument.

Crime and Tort

Here our concern is with the criminal prosecution of an offender. There may be a civil remedy against him also, but this will usually be in the realm of tort. (There are exceptions, *e.g.* Common Assault, where a criminal conviction bans a civil action). Often, unfortunately, a civil remedy is of little use to the victim in practice. Note that under the *Theft Act* a court may award restitution, and grant a Compensation Order under the *Criminal Courts Act*.

Procedure (outline)

1. A summary offence is one triable solely by magistrates. These are set out in Schedule 1 to the *1977 Criminal Law Act*.

2. An offence triable on Indictment only will be heard by judge and jury in the Crown Court. The statement of offence read out to the defendant is known as "The Indictment."

3. Schedule 3 of the 1977 Act sets out offences which are triable either way. It is up to the magistrates to decide which form of trial is appropriate, but the accused must consent to a summary hearing.

The Burden of Proof

"Throughout the web of English Criminal Law, one golden thread is always to be seen—that it is the duty of the prosecution to prove the prisoner's guilt . . . If at the end of, and on the whole of the case, there is a reasonable doubt, created by the evidence given by either the prosecution or the prisoner, as to whether the prisoner [killed the deceased] the prosecution has not made out the case and the prisoner is entitled to an acquittal:" Lord Sankey L.C. in *Woolmington* v. *D.P.P.* (1935).

Thus the prosecution must prove each of the elements of the offence. If, however, the defendant admits that he performed the act in question but denies his responsibility because he lacked the *actus reus* (*i.e.* he was an automaton); or the *mens rea* (*e.g.* was mistaken); or he claims a defence (*e.g.* self defence), then he must adduce some evidence of this: the *Evidential Burden*. Once he has satisfied this burden, the burden of proof again returns to the prosecution.

Exceptionally, the burden of proof is cast upon the defence, *e.g.* on a claim of insanity. Here the burden is to prove such facts "*on the balance of probabilities*" and not beyond reasonable doubt.

Criminal Justice Act 1967 s. 8:

> "A court or jury in determining whether a person has committed an offence,
> (a) shall not be bound in law to infer that he intended or foresaw a result of his actions by reason only of its being a natural and probable consequence of these actions; but
> (b) shall decide whether he did intend or foresee that result by reference to all the evidence drawing such inferences from the evidence as appear proper in the circumstances."

The test of intention and foresight is thus subjective, though this was not always so. (See, *e.g. D.P.P.* v. *Andrews*). Section 8 is only relevant if the constituents of a crime require that intention or foresight need be proved, (see infra., *D.P.P.* v. *Majewski*).

CHAPTER 1

PRELIMINARY CONCEPTS

The Crown must show that the accused brought about a state of affairs forbidden by the criminal law (the *actus reus*) and that at the time, he possessed the necessary state of mind towards that act, or its consequences (the *mens rea*). The defendant may admit both, but deny liability because he has a "defence" ("I did hit X intentionally, but I thought that he was going to kill me"). Generally speaking, motive ("I hit him because he insulted my sister") will not be relevant.

(a) Actus Reus

This is all the elements of a crime except those relating to the accused's state of mind. If there is no *actus reus*, there is no crime. Thus in attempt, the *actus reus* will be carrying out a series of acts sufficiently proximate to the completion of the crime, in conspiracy, coming to an agreement.

It is argued, however, that there must be some mental element in the actus, *i.e.* the state of affairs constituting an actus must be as a result of *willed conduct*, thus if D injures P simply as a result of accidentally falling over, there is no willed assault; likewise where X pushes D's hand into P's face, or D suffers a "spasm" which causes him to hit P. Here, D is an "automaton," not in control of his actions. It would seem that automatism is not therefore a true "defence" as D has no need of one—there has been no *actus*. (See *Hill* v. *Baxter* (1958).) D may still be liable, however, if he has deliberately put himself in the position where he may react in such a way. Thus D, knowing he suffers from epilepsy, drives a car and causes an accident. Here it seems sound to say that his putting himself in such a position is the willed *actus reus* which causes the accident.

Quare where D is too drunk to will an *actus* but physically causes one; see *Majewski* v. *D.P.P.*, *infra*.

R. v. *Dadson* (1850)

D was guarding a copse when he saw P, who had stolen some wood, running away. P failed to stop at D's call so D shot him. D was charged with shooting with intent to cause grievous bodily harm. The court accepted that such conduct might be justifiable if D had stopped an "escaping felon," *i.e.* a person with convictions for such offences. P had such convictions, but D did not know of them. D was convicted.

The case has been criticised as lacking an *actus reus*, *i.e.* D *was* shooting an escaping felon, which is no crime. However, the *actus reus* is *not* shooting at a man who is not an escaping felon, but simply shooting at a man. This D did. He also intended to shoot, and is thus liable unless he can bring himself within a defence. The defence of arresting an escaping felon is not open to D as a defendant must know of facts that constitute a defence. Thus if I shoot you and you, unknown to me, were about to shoot me, I cannot claim "self-defence" as I did not know of facts which, objectively, seem to give me a defence.

R. v. *Deller* (1952)

D was charged with obtaining one motor car by the false pretence that he had a right to sell another, that other being "free from incumbrances." D had, however, signed an agreement to mortgage his car which, if valid, would have deprived D of the right to sell or exchange it. There would have been no doubt about D's liability had the prior "mortgage" been legally enforceable, but it was invalid. Because of this, and completely unknown to D, his car actually was "free of encumbrances" when he sold it. D's conviction was quashed. Note that the *actus reus* is obtaining by false pretences. Here, by chance, the pretences are true. D intended to commit an illegal act but, by chance, nothing he did or said was illegal.

N.B. D is *not* setting up a defence—he does not need to, there is no *actus reus* to defend.

Could D have been charged with an attempt? (*Infra*, see *Haughton* v. *Smith*).

Causation

It must be proved that D's act caused any consequences implicit in the *actus reus*. Thus, *e.g.* in murder, it must be proved that D's assault caused the death. Note that firstly the act must cause the result in fact, and then in law. The second is narrower; thus if I invite you to dinner at 8.00 p.m. and you are injured by a bus outside my door at 7.55 p.m. I may have partly caused your injury in fact, but not in law.

In *R.* v. *White* (1910) D put cyanide into his mother's drink intending to kill her. She was found dead later having sipped from the glass, but medical evidence showed that she died from a heart attack and not the poison. D, therefore, was found guilty of only attempted murder.

In *R.* v. *Hensler* (1870) D wrote a begging letter to P, pretending to be a poor widow. P was not deceived, but sent the money in order to trap D. One may say that *in fact* D was a cause of this result, as it would not have happened without his letter, but *in law* the direct cause test is not satisfied. Examine the offence; obtaining by false pretences. The pretences must deceive P, who will give to D. The pretences did not succeed; P gave the money for another reason, thus it was not the "pretences" that "obtained." D was convicted of an attempt.

Where D has directly caused a series of events which result in harm to P, the courts are loath to say that an extraneous event has broken the chain of causation, unless the event is wholly unconnected with the original incident. Thus if D puts a victim in such fear that P is injured in escaping from him, D will be liable (*R.* v. *Halliday*, *infra*).

R. v. *Smith* (1959)

D wounded P in a fight involving several other soldiers. The medical orderly was extremely pressed due to "near battle conditions" and P received what would, in normal circumstances, have been grossly negligent treatment. Considering the occasion, the treatment was understandable and D was found guilty of murder. The Court distinguished *R.* v. *Jordan* as there it appeared that D may have died not from the wounds, but from "palpably wrong" treatment. The Court of Appeal had felt constrained to quash Jordan's conviction on hearing the new evidence establishing this, but note their very guarded words. The test is; has the original injury, albeit badly treated, caused the injury, or is there a completely new cause? *Jordan* is undoubtedly the exception, as can be seen in:

R. v. *Blaue* (1975)

D was convicted of manslaughter. As a result of his attack on a child, a blood transfusion was essential to save her life. The child's parents, being Jehovah's Witnesses refused permission for this on religous grounds. D's conviction was upheld. D must take his victim as he finds him, and though a wholly unreasonable refusal of treatment might break the chain of causation, religous beliefs cannot constitute that.

What if a victim refused treatment because "I will only be treated by white Anglo-Saxon doctors" and none was available, the patient therefore dying?

Omissions

An omission may constitute an actus, but only where D is under a duty to perform the act omitted, thus Winfield's spectator watching the drowning of an unknown child in two feet of water is not criminally liable. The duty may be by law—*e.g.* parent and child—or by agreement—*e.g.* an employment contract. (See *R.* v. *Pitwood*, *infra*). Thus if Winfield's observer had been the father of the child, or a lifeguard under contract to patrol the beach, he would doubtless be guilty of manslaughter. It is difficult to imagine liability for crimes other than those of negligence coming about by omission (see "Manslaughter," *infra*).

Perhaps the most curious omission case is *Fagan* v. *M.P.C.* (1968). D accidentally placed his car on a policeman's foot, but deliberately omitted to remove it. The court held that the assault was a "continuing act."

Lastly consider *R.* v. *Larsonneur* (1933) D was convicted under the 1920 Aliens Order for being present in the U.K. being a prohibited alien. D was brought to this country not by her voluntary will, but under force by the police. This "state of affairs" decision has been universally condemned, though one can argue that the physical movements which caused D to be here were willed, *i.e.* not the acts of an automaton. However, the judgment of Lord Hewart C.J. shows no real discussion of either the *actus* or *mens,* and it is best treated as exceptional.

(b) Mens Rea

I.e. the "guilty mind" that must accompany the criminal act. Note the *mens rea* does not require an "evil" mind, a man's motive may be good or bad. *Mens rea* is usually described as consisting of four heads.

1. *Intention*

Broadly, intention is of two types. First, those objects which D *desires* to bring about, and subsequently tries to; secondly, those which he does not desire to bring about, but he recognises that he must bring them about in order to achieve whatever he does desire. Thus if D decides to shoot at P through a closed window, breaking the window is a condition precedent to obtaining his desired end (hitting P). It thus seems reasonable to say that he intends to break the window. (Sometimes known as "oblique intention.")

This has been applied to the case where D blows up an aeroplane intending to collect the insurance money on one of the passengers. However, as collecting the money is no part of the *actus reus* of murder, this seems best ignored as purely motive. The direct intention is to kill P, and perhaps destroying the plane is the "oblique intent." There must obviously be a line drawn between those consequences which are certain to result from D's action, and those which may result. Where D *desired* the consequences, the fact that that result is merely possible does not matter, if it in fact happens. Thus if I desire to harm you when I shoot, the fact that I have only a 100 to 1 chance of hitting you does not prevent my having the intention of hitting you. If, on the other hand, I do not desire a consequence, but realise that it is something less than "virtually certain" or "highly probable," then I do not intend that consequence (See Lord Hailsham in *Hyam* v. *D.P.P.*).

2. *Recklessness*

This involves the voluntary acceptance by D that a forbidden consequence may result from his actions, yet he goes on nevertheless. The consequence must not be virtually certain, and it must not be desired. All that is necessary is the realisation by D that his actions *risk* bringing about the illegal consequence, thus if D does not foresee what might happen, he is not reckless.

If D, when driving down a road at 80 m.p.h. sees an old lady in the road and thinks "there is an old lady," that, in itself, is not recklessness. When he thinks "I suppose I might hit her if I carry on, oh dear!" and does not slow down, he is reckless, for then he accepts the risk of hitting her. He will not be saved from liability by saying that he did not wish to hit her. Note that recklessness is a *relative* standard. The surgeon performing an operation to save life may lawfully accept *some* risk; the man shooting his pistol for fun will not be allowed to take *any* risk at all.

3. *Negligence*

Here the test is objective; would a reasonable man have realised that there was some risk involved? Crimes of negligence are few, the most important being manslaughter by gross negligence. There are, however, elements of other crimes that require consideration of negligence, *e.g.* the "reasonable mistake" test. Note that there are really two different ways of classifying the reasonable man test:
(i) Would a hypothetical reasonable man divorced from the circumstances of the accused have seen the risk; (ii) would the accused, with all his peculiarities, if *he* had acted as a reasonable man, have seen the risk.

English law has generally adopted the former test, but note *D.P.P.* v. *Camplin* (*infra*).

N.B. Take care in reading old cases; often judges use the

word "reckless" to mean a form of gross negligence, or "objective" recklessness.

4. *Blameless Inadvertence*

Neither D, nor any reasonable man, could have anticipated the harm that came about from D's actions.

For the majority of crimes, liability will be grounded whether the accused intended the result or was reckless. Negligence is usually not enough. The academic theory can seem strained when examining decisions. Note, *e.g.* Lord Hailsham's wide definition of intention in *Hyam*.

In *R.* v. *Steane* (1947) D appealed against his conviction under the Defence Regulations for "doing acts with intent to assist the enemy." Forced through torture, D agreed to make propaganda broadcasts for the Nazis. His appeal was allowed, Lord Goddard C.J. stating that D's intent was to save his family, not aid the enemy. However, D did intend to do the acts which constituted the *actus reus* (make the broadcast), knowing that such broadcasts would aid the enemy. It would have been more conceptually sound for the court to have acknowledged the existence of *mens rea*, but allowed the defence of duress to negate D's liability.

How does the Court's approach differ in *D.P.P.* v. *Chandler* (1962)?

Ulterior or Specific Intent

For some crimes there is a further requirement beyond the actus and mens—a specific intent. Thus in a murder trial, the crown must prove the physical act that killed (*actus*), that D intended the blow (*mens*) and that by that blow he intended a certain consequence, namely to cause P death or g.b.h. (specific intent). Thus generally, the *mens* relates to the act, and the specific intent to its consequences.

Recently, the term has also been applied to statutory offences requiring more than simply the intention to commit a physical act. Thus in theft, the accused must intend that by his act he permanently deprives someone; in burglary under section 9 (1) (*a*), the prosecution must show that D entered as a trespasser intending to commit a particular offence. Students should not trouble themselves by attempting to see "both types" of specific intent as belonging to the same group, as this will only lead to confusion.

What if D drives around looking for P, intending to run him over and thereby kill him and, while looking, he realises that he has run over someone (who turns out to be P)? Throughout the time of his *actus*, D intended to kill P. He is not guilty of murder if P dies, however, for despite intending to kill (specific intent) he did not have *mens rea* in relation to the physical act of killing, *i.e.* running P over, as regards which he was only negligent.

Question: For murder, broadly speaking, the accused must kill, intend the blow and intend that it kill or cause g.b.h. For rape, the accused must have intercourse without consent, intend the intercourse, and further intend that it be without consent. Murder is a crime of specific intent, rape is not. Why not? (See "Drunkenness," *infra*.)

(c) Transferred Malice

The traditional theory that the *actus* and *mens* must coincide is not absolute. What if D shoots at X intending to kill him, but misses and kills Y? It would be ludicrous for X to escape liability, but the *mens* was in relation to X, and the *actus*, to Y. To circumvent this problem, the courts developed the doctrine of Transferred Malice, whereby the intent to harm X is transferred to Y if D injures Y. Thus a charge might read "D caused grevious bodily harm to Y with intent to injure X."

In *R.* v. *Latimer* (1886), D aimed a blow with his belt at P, intending to cause some small injury, however the belt hit and severely injured Y. D was held guilty of the unlawful wounding of Y.

If D's *mens rea* is that of a different crime to the *actus reus* he causes, he cannot be convicted. Thus in *R*. v. *Pembliton* (1874), where D threw a stone at a group of people and broke a window, his conviction was quashed. The *actus reus* was of criminal damage, but the *mens rea*, of assault.

Where the *mens rea* of one crime necessarily includes the *mens rea* of a lesser crime, the malice may be transferred. So if D shoots intending to kill P but causes grevious bodily harm to X, or a simple assault to Y, he may be convicted of that lesser offence, as anyone who shoots intending to kill obviously intends to cause g.b.h., and to assault.

N.B. Any question involving transferred malice usually requires consideration of the following:

(i) Can the malice be transferred, *i.e.* are the *actus* and *mens* of the same crime?

(ii) Was D reckless in relation to the *actus reus* actually caused? If so he may still be guilty even though the malice cannot be transferred.

(iii) Can D be liable for attempt in relation to the crime for which he has *mens rea*?

(d) Non-Coincidence of Actus and Mens in Time

What if D tries to kill P and, thinking P dead, disposes of the "body," when in fact, P was still alive and the "disposal" kills him? The problem here is that when D possesses the *mens rea* of murder, he causes only bodily harm. When he commits the *actus reus* of homicide, he has no *mens rea* as he believes he is disposing of a corpse. Should this technical non-coincidence excuse D? The leading case is *Thabo Meli* v. *R.* (1954).

D planned to kill P and attacked him, but it was the disposal of P's body which, unknown to D, was still alive, that actually killed P. The House of Lords upheld D's conviction for murder, Lord Reid stating that

"It appears to their lordships impossible to divide up what was really one series of acts in this way ... There is no doubt that the accused set out to do all these acts in order to achieve their plan ..."

Note the emphasis on the pre-arranged plan. Does this mean that if D attacks P on the spur of the moment, and subsequently causes the death when disposing of the "corpse" that he cannot be convicted of murder?

Guidance is found in *R.* v. *Church* (1965). Here D was taunted by a prostitute for failing to have intercourse with her. As a result, he knocked her unconscious and, thinking her dead, threw the "body" into a river. P died of drowning. At his trial the judge told the jury that they might only convict of murder if satisfied that D did not believe P dead when he threw her into the river. On appeal (rather hopefully!), Edmund Davies L.J. states that this direction:

"Was unduly benevolent to the appellant, and the jury should have been told that it was still open to them to convict of murder notwithstanding that the appellant may have thought [P dead] when he threw her body into the river as *a series of acts designed to cause death or grievous bodily harm.*"

Note that, if followed, this remark would extend Meli in two important respects; (i) doing away with the necessity for a pre-arranged plan, and (ii) entailing a conviction for murder even though D does not intend to kill by his "series of acts" but intends merely g.b.h. Quare where D recognises only the "risk" of g.b.h.? (*Infra*, "Murder").

(e) Strict Liability

This refers to crimes which require no consideration of the accused's *mens rea*. It is NOT synonymous with "blameless inadvertence," as it is not a head of *mens rea*. *Mens rea* is irrelevant. As a matter of practice, however, it will often be the case that D was blameless, otherwise whether or not a crime is one of strict liability would be irrelevant.

In *R.* v. *Prince*, D was charged with taking a girl under 16 out of the possession of her parents. It was held to be irrelevant that D honestly, and reasonably, believed her to be over 16.

Such crimes are almost all statutory and a defence of the Court's attitude is difficult. Note that in *Prince* the age border-line is an arbitrary one. These offences, however are not absolute. Thus, had Prince believed P not to be in her parents possession, he would not have been convicted (See *R.* v. *Hibbert* (1869)).

Courts have differed as to whether the absence of the word "knowingly" ought to be decisive. (See *Cundy* v. *Le Cocq*, 1884; *Sherras* v. *De Rutzen* (1895)).

N.B. Though an offence may be one of strict liability, are aiding and abetting it, or attempting it, themselves such offences? (*Infra*.)

(f) Vicarious Liability

This doctrine fixes criminal liability on X for acts committed by Y. As in tort, the main concern is with the employment situation, though there is no general principle of vicarious liability in criminal law. (*R.* v. *Huggins* (1730).)

N.B. This is NOT the same as strict liability. Unless the offence is *also* one of strict liability, the prosecution must show that the employee had the requisite *mens rea*.

The Courts have employed the "Delegation Principle" to fix an employer with liability, where D has delegated responsibility for performance of a statutory duty to his employees, *e.g. Allen* v. *Whitehead* (1930) (prostitutes gathering in café where D left a manager in control for eight days). Whether a partial delegation is enough is uncertain; see *Vane* v. *Yianiopellos* (1965).

Also important is the situation concerning consumer sales, where it is important to prosecute the shopowner and not the errand boy. (See, *e.g. Coppen* v. *Moore* [No. 2] (1898).) Many statutes now provide for an employer to have a defence if he can show that he has taken all reasonable care. Note also the liability of Corporations, particularly through Lord Haldane's "Organic Theory" where a company policy can be traced to the "directing mind" of the firm. (See *Bolton* v. *Graham* (1957).)

CHAPTER 2

ACCOMPLICES

"Whosoever shall aid, abet, counsel or procure the commission of any indictable offence whether the same be an offence at common law or by virtue of any act passed or to be passed, shall be liable to be tried, indicted and punished as a principal offender" (*Accessories and Abettors Act, 1861*, as amended).

1. It is in order to charge D simply with "aiding, abetting, counselling or procuring."

2. A pre-requisite to liability is the commission of an offence by the principal. If the counselled crime does not take place, the charge is "Inciting."

3. If D abets a principal who is legally incapable of committing a crime, *e.g.* a child under 10 years old, then D is guilty as principal, through the child's innocent agency. Thus if D counsels X, a six year old, to steal, D is guilty of theft, and the child an innocent agent.

4. Care must be taken in reading old cases, where secondary parties to felonies were known as "principals in the second degree" or "accessories before the fact." Such terms are now obsolete.

5. One who aids *after* the crime is not an accomplice. He must be charged under the *Criminal Law Act 1967* (*infra*).

6. "Aid and abet" and "counsel and procure" are terms of art. They must be interpreted through cases, not dictionaries.

Abettors

A person who "aids and abets" is present at the time of commission of the offence, and assists or encourages the principal. There is obviously a borderline with the position where D^1 and D^2 are both principals, *e.g.* if D^1 holds P while D^2 kills him, both are principals to murder.

Mere presence at the time of the crime is not enough. Thus in *R. v. Coney* (1882) D's conviction was quashed due to a direction by the trial chairman that his presence at a prize fight was conclusive evidence of aiding and abetting (though it was prima facie evidence). In *R. v. Clarkson* (1971) the convictions of D^1 and D^2 were quashed after they were convicted of abetting rape by watching, but taking no active part.

> "There must be an intention to encourage, and there must be encouragement in fact, in such cases as the present case,"

per Megaw L.J.

So in *R. v. Baldesserre* (1930) D was found guilty of abetting manslaughter which occurred as a result of X's reckless driving, when he was present in the car encouraging X to drive in such a manner. Note *Wilcox v. Jeffery* (1951), where D was convicted of aiding Z to give illegal musical performances, when he attended the performance, applauded and reported it. Lord Goddard C.J., seems to be implying that it was D's duty to protest at the unlawful performance.

Counsellors

A counsellor is one who, before a crime is committed, advises its commission or gives other assistance to the principal.

In *R.* v. *Fretwell* (1862) D produced an abortificient for a pregnant woman. The woman took the drug and died. D was held not to be guilty of being an accessory to self murder, as he merely procured the drug because of the woman's suicide threats, and hoped that she would not use it. This decision is probably over-generous to the accused. More representative is *N.C.B.* v. *Gamble* (1959) where a weighbridge operator was found guilty when he realised that a lorry was overloaded, but still handed the driver a ticket in order for him to drive away. This decision appears to be based on the fact that the operator did have the right to refuse to give the ticket to the driver. Had the N.C.B. led evidence to show that the operator did not realise this, they would probably have been acquitted.

N.B. this case does NOT concern vicarious liability, the N.C.B. themselves requested that they be treated as the defendant). In *R.* v. *Lomas* (1913) D was held not liable as an accessory to burglary where he returned a jemmy to P (principal offender). The case has been seen as implying that D must know of the particular crime P has in mind, however Devlin J. in *Gamble* states that Lomas was not liable as he was returning to P what P would otherwise have a civil law right to reclaim. (Is this realistic?)

In *R.* v. *Bainbridge* (1959), D provided P with cutting equipment and, though D did not know the precise crime that P was about to commit, his conviction was upheld as he knew the "type of crime." (The jury must be taken to have rejected D's story that he believed the equipment would be used for cutting-up stolen goods). This case necessarily begs the question "when is a crime of the same type as another?"

What if there are unforeseen consequences?

D will be liable where these follow from a joint enterprise, unless P has substantially varied the plan. Thus if P, in the course of a fight, produces a knife of which D knew nothing and kills X, D may be liable for common assault but not for abetting murder; *Davies* v. *D.P.P.* (1954).

In *R.* v. *Saunders and Archer* (1576) D procured a poisoned apple for P to give to his wife. The apple was given by the wife, in P's presence, to their child, who died. D was held not guilty of being an accessory to murder by P. This is because P, having created the danger, was under a duty to snatch the apple from the child. Thus the result is as if P deliberately set out to kill a third party with the apple provided for his wife. If P had not been present at the incident, then the risk of the child's death would have been on P and D.

Is murder of the child the "same type of crime" as murder of the wife? Is then, *Saunders* consistent with dicta in *Bainbridge*?

What if P is acquitted?

D cannot be guilty where there has been no crime committed by P (*Thornton* v. *Mitchell* (1940)). This must be contrasted with the position where P has committed an offence, but has a defence.

Thus in *R.* v. *Bourne* (1952) where D forced his wife to have intercourse with an alsation dog, D was convicted of abetting this buggery. It was assumed that P would have had a defence of duress had she been charged. It therefore seems that P committed the *actus reus*, had the *mens rea* (intention) to commit it, but could rely on a defence as she was forced to commit it.

In *R.* v. *Cogan and Leak* (1975) C was convicted of raping L's wife, and L of abetting him. C's conviction was questioned in the Court of Appeal as the trial judge had wrongly directed that his belief in consent need be reasonable. (*Cf. Morgan* v. *D.P.P.*, *infra*). The court strained to uphold the conviction of L, however, by employing the doctrine of innocent agency. Note that here, unlike *Bourne,* C does not have the requisite *mens rea*, but has merely performed the *actus reus*.

It would seem more satisfactory nevertheless to convict L of abetting this *actus reus* than to employ the innocent agency doctrine, which necessarily involve charging C with the rape of his own wife. This approach could lead to ludicrous results where, *e.g.* D aids a principal who commits the *actus reus* of bigamy!

The courts are, unfortunately, loath to add D's *mens rea* to P's *actus reus*. In *R.* v. *Richards* (Isabelle) (1973) D counselled two men to cause g.b.h. to her husband. This they did, though they were convicted of causing only a.b.h. (Section 20 *O.A.P.A. 1861*). The prosecution argued that D should be guilty of abetting the more serious offence under section 18 as she intended the g.b.h., and the *actus reus* of this offence, being the same as that under section 20, had been caused. This argument was rejected, though the court placed much emphasis on the fact that D was some distance away from where the assault took place.

Assistant Offenders

Section 4 and section 5 of the *Criminal Law Act 1967* replace the old offences of being "an accessory after the fact" and of "compounding or misprision of felony."

Section 4 (1):

> "Where a person has committed an arrestable offence, any other person who knowing or believing him to be guilty of the offence or of some other arrestable offence, does without lawful authority or reasonable excuse any act with intent to impede his apprehension or prosecution shall be guilty of an offence . . ."

Lyle J. :

> "There is no foundation for the contention [that the prosecution needs to prove that the accused knew who committed the offence] and that he did an act in relation to that person. What has to be proved is as follows, first, it must be proved that a person has committed an arrestable offence; second, that another person knew or believed that the first had committed it; third, that the second person did an act

with intent to impede the apprehension or prosecution of the first person . . .;" *R.* v. *Brindley and Long* (1970). Thus the bystander who witnesses a robbery and then sends a police car in the wrong direction, is guilty under section 4.

Section 5 makes it an offence to accept or agree to accept some consideration in return for failing to disclose information. This requires:

 (i) Proof of the commission of an arrestable offence;
 (ii) D's knowledge or belief that it has been committed;
(iii) D's belief that he has valuable information;
(iv) D's acceptance of consideration, except by way of compensation.

CHAPTER 3

INCHOATE OFFENCES

(a) Incitement

The incitement of another to commit an indictable offence is itself a crime: *R.* v. *Higgins* (1801). It was assumed in *R.* v. *Curr* (1967) that an incitement to commit a summary offence is also triable on indictment but this is now overruled by the *Criminal Law Act 1977* s. 15 (1) *(b)*, thus incitement to commit a summary offence is itself only triable summarily.

The person incited need not be swayed by the arguments of D, neither is there a requirement that the crime need actually be committed. If, however, the inciting words do not reach the intended principal, *e.g.* because of a failure in the post or because that other is deaf, then an attempt to incite might be charged.

In *R*. v. *Curr*, D organised women to collect social security benefit to which they were not entitled. He was acquitted as there was no evidence put forward to show that the women had sufficient *mens rea* for the offence. This result has been criticised, opinion seeming to be that it ought to have been enough to prove that D thought that the women had the requisite *mens rea*.

If I mislead X into committing an act which I know to be criminal, but he does not, as he is not in possession of certain facts known to me, then this is not incitement. Thus if I persuade X to remove a case by telling him (falsely) that I have permission to remove it, I have not incited theft. I would, however, seem to be guilty of theft by the doctrine of innocent agency.

It seems not to be relevant that the crime incited is impossible. This follows from *R*. v. *McDonough* (1962). Here D was convicted of inciting P to remove stolen carcases, though there was no evidence to show that any such carcases had been stolen at the relevant time. This seems supportable on the understanding that D believed that the carcases existed at the time.

However, in *Haughton* v. *Smith* (*infra*), the House of Lords laid down the rule that an attempt to commit a crime which is itself impossible of commission is not an offence. One might argue that logically, the same rule should apply to incitement and conspiracy to do the impossible. From *D.P.P.* v. *Nock* (*infra*) it is clear that the rule does apply to conspiracy, unfortunately Lord Scarman in that case stated that *McDonough* was a correct decision as the *actus reus*, the making of the incitement, was complete. One problem here is that the *actus reus* of conspiracy, the agreement, was also complete in that case, yet the House of Lords unanimously held it not to be an indictable conspiracy. The position here must, therefore, be regarded as unclear.

(b) Attempt

It is an indictable offence to attempt to commit any indictable offence, and by the *Powers of Criminal Courts Act,* s. 18 (2) the attempt is punishable in the same way as the substantive offence.

(a) Mens Rea

The prosecution must prove that accused *intended* to bring about the crime contemplated. When any consequence is implicit in the definition of the crime (*e.g.* in murder, that the act caused a death) it must be shown that the accused intended that consequence. Thus it is NOT true to say that the *mens rea* of attempt is the same as that of the completed crime, as this latter often involves a lesser *mens, e.g.* recklessness will usually suffice. While it is true, then, to say that D may be guilty of murder by virtue of his intending g.b.h., only an intention to kill will ground attempted murder—*R.* v. *Whybrow* (1951).

Likewise, though D will be guilty of assault if he is reckless as to whether he strikes P, he will only be guilty of attempted assault if he intended the blow. He may be guilty, however, if he is merely reckless as to the circumstances. It has been argued that where, *e.g.* D tries to pick up an article thinking "even if this is not mine, I'll keep it," and is stopped by the owner, D is still guilty of attempted theft as he intended to take the article, and was reckless only as to the circumstances. It might be argued, alternatively, that section 1 of the *Theft Act* requires that D appropriate "property belonging to another." As D is only reckless as to whether he takes property belonging to another, he does not "intend" a crucial part of the *actus reus* of theft, and should not, therefore, be guilty of an attempt.

Strict Liability

It will be remembered that aiding and abetting being a common law offence, where D aids the commission of an offence of strict liability, he must be shown to have *mens rea* in relation to the abetting. Logically, as attempt is a common law offence, the same should be true here.

Authority is, however, scant in this area. Much has been made of the Assize case, *R.* v. *Collier* (1960). D was charged with attempting intercourse with a girl under 16, contrary to the *Sexual Offences Act*. By section 6 of the Act, a defendant has a defence where he, *inter alia*, believes the girl to be over 16. As the accused fitted the terms of the defence, Streatfield J. allowed him to take advantage of the defence on the attempt charge. The academic argument is that this is incorrect. Even though the offence was one of strict liability (*R.* v. *Prince*, *supra*) attempting the offence is not. D must be shown to have *mens rea*, which, in this case, he did not have. Consequently D ought not to have needed the defence.

It is submitted, however, that this is reading more in the decision than the judge intended. Preferable is *Gardner* v. *Akeroyd* (1952), which is support for the view that *mens rea* is required here.

(b) Actus Reus

Despite earlier rulings that almost any act done with intent to commit a crime was an offence, it was settled in *R.* v. *Eagleton* (1855) that an accused will only be liable where his acts are sufficiently proximate to its completion. A modern exception is *R.* v. *Gurmit Singh* (1966). Here D procured a stamp in order to forge documents. Though D had not gone sufficiently far to be convicted of an attempt, McNair J. held that he was guilty of procuring with intent to defraud. Were this decision to be followed, almost any act of preparation would be indictable, though it would seem that *Singh* has largely been ignored by the courts. To be sufficiently proximate, D must be well on the way to committing the full crime. In *R.* v. *Robinson* (1915) D tied himself up, called the police and pretended to have been robbed in order to collect insurance money. His conviction for attempting to obtain by false pretences was quashed.

In *R*. v. *Button* (1900) D deceived the organisers of a race into granting him a handicap by pretending to be one Sims, who was a poor runner. As D went to collect his prize the fraud was discovered and he was arrested. He was convicted of attempting to obtain by false pretences.

The clue to reconciling these cases is to examine the offences charged, *i.e.* obtaining by false pretences. Button had almost reached his goal, he had deceived those from whom he was to obtain. Robinson, on the other hand, could only collect the money from the insurance company. Though his deceiving the police officer was a preparatory step, he was far from deceiving those from whom he was to obtain. (Note also *Commer* v. *Bloomfield* (1970) which must be considered near the border-line.)

Attempts have been made to try to find a principal to determine at what point D's preparation becomes an indictable attempt, but none has been completely successful. The "Equivocality Theory" held D liable where his actions:

> "cannot reasonably be regarded as having any other purpose other than the commission of *that specific crime*."

This was given judicial approval in England in *Davey* v. *Lee* (1967), where the defendants were caught breaking into a compound, and convicted of attempting to steal copper. The difficulty of applying the theory is highlighted in this case; the defendants acts could have been preliminary to other crimes, *e.g.* office breaking, and were not, thus, unequivocal.

Convictions in *Campbell and Bradley* v. *Ward* (1955), a New Zealand case, were quashed as the defendants acts of getting into cars did not unequivocally indicate their stated intention of stealing car batteries. This rather peculiar result the English courts refused to follow, where the accused's stated intention appeared to negate liability for his equivocal act (*Jones* v. *Brooks* (1968)). The test appears to find little judicial support now.

Attempting the Impossible

Care must be taken in distinguishing what is *physically* impossible (D cannot complete the *actus reus* due to some outside contingency, *e.g.* the pocket he picks is empty) and what is *legally* impossible (D *can* perform the *actus reus* but, because of facts not known to him, this turns out not to constitute the *actus reus* of a crime.

Such a case is *Haughton* v. *Smith* (1973).

A van loaded with stolen tins was captured by the police. It was allowed on its way, with the addition of two officers, and rendezvoused with D, who unloaded the tins. D was not charged with handling stolen goods, as the prosecution admitted that the goods had been reduced into lawful custody, and were no longer stolen. (This point is *not* part of the decision, indeed Lord Hailsham queried whether or not this concession should have been made.) Instead, D was charged with attempting to receive goods, which by then were not stolen. The House of Lords held that such an indictment could not stand. Note Lord Hailsham's division (following Turner J.) of attempts into six categories.

> *N.B.:* "*Third* (D) may be prevented by some outside agency from doing some act necessary to complete commission of the crime . . . *Fourth* he may fail . . . through ineptitude, inefficiency or insufficient means . . . *Fifth* he may find that what he is proposing to do is after all impossible, not because of insufficiency of means but because it is for some reason physically not possible . . . *Sixth* he may without interruption efficiently do every act which he has set out to do, but may be saved from criminal liability by the fact that what he has done, contrary to his own belief at the time, does not after all amount in law, to a crime."

Thus *Smith* is a case of legal impossibility—D was able to carry out the whole *actus*, *i.e.* remove the tins from the van, and, contrary to his own belief, this act was not illegal. Their Lordships also held (*obiter*) that cases of attempt within the fifth category (physical impossibility) are no longer indictable. Thus *R.* v. *Ring* (1872), where D was convicted of attempting to steal from an empty pocket, is disapproved of by Lord Reid.

In *Partington* v. *Williams* (1976) it was held following this *obiter*, that on a charge of attempted theft from any empty wallet, the conviction must be quashed. This may now be doubted because of the conspiracy case, *D.P.P.* v. *Nock*. Here Lord Diplock stated that, provided the indictment is drawn in suitably broad terms, such a defendant ought to be convicted, and Lord Scarman agreed. It may be that in future decisions, *Smith* will be confined to legal impossibility, though it must be admitted that it is by no means easy to reconcile what is said in *Nock* with some of the decisions their lordships purport to be agreeing with. Obviously, any student must read both *Smith* and *Nock* carefully.

(c) Conspiracy

Conspiracy was, of course, a common law offence. The *Criminal Law Act 1977* creates a new offence of Statutory Conspiracy. It also abolishes much of the common law offence, but preserves conspiracy to defraud and conspiracy to corrupt public morals or outrage public decency. Statutory Conspiracy covers conspiracies to commit any criminal offence, whether triable on indictment or summarily, thus, in the latter case, it is an indictable conspiracy to conspire to commit a summary offence (though prosecution here requires the comment of the D.P.P.) Indictable conspiracies therefore comprise:

(i) conspiracy to commit any criminal offence ("statutory conspiracy")

(ii) conspiracy to defraud (common law);

(iii) conspiracy to corrupt public morals or outrage public decency (common law) *except* where the agreement is to commit an existing criminal offence, *e.g.* under the *Obscene Publications Act*, when the relevant statutory conspiracy should be charged.

As regards conspiracy to defraud, this is preserved by section 5 (2). Thus it seems that when D^1 and D^2 agree to obtain by deception, the offence is conspiracy to defraud. There is, it would seem, no such offence as "conspiracy to obtain by deception per section 15 of the Theft Act." Likewise, conspiracy to steal is no offence, as facts grounding that offence must amount to conspiracy to defraud. It is not clear whether this necessarily applies to *all Theft Act* offences, *e.g.* is a "conspiracy to handle" a conspiracy to defraud? Judicial decision is awaited.

N.B. Where facts indicate a conspiracy to corrupt public morals which also amounts to conspiracy to commit a statutory offence, the only charge is the *statutory* conspiracy. Where facts indicating conspiracy to defraud also amount to conspiracy to commit a statutory offence, *e.g.* theft, the only charge is *conspiracy to defraud*.

The *actus reus* of conspiracy is the *agreement*, thus the parties must be beyond the stage of negotiation (*R.* v. *Walker* (1962)). The *mens rea* is the intention to carry out that agreement.

It has been the practice of prosecutors to charge conspiracy where the evidence shows contact between certain of the defendants only. Thus in the so-called "Wheel conspiracy" D^1 agrees with D^2, who agrees with D^3, etc., to perform the criminal act. This seems unobjectionable where each is agreeing to an enterprise to be entered into by all. In *R.* v. *Meyrick* (1929), however, D^1 and D^2 made separate agreements with a police officer, intending only to benefit themselves individually (each wanted the police to keep away from his own Soho nightclub). The defendants were convicted. A better decision is *R.* v. *Griffiths* (1965), where a number of farmers agreed with D^1 to defraud the Ministry of Agriculture: each agreeing purely to a separate personal fraud. The Court of Appeal declared this not to be a conspiracy between all the participants. Paull J. stated:

> "It must be shown that the alleged conspirators were acting in pursuance of a criminal purpose held in common between them."

Statutory Conspiracy

Criminal Law Act 1977 s. 1 (1):

> ". . . if a person agrees with any other person or persons that a course of conduct shall be pursued which will *necessarily* amount to or involve the commission of any offence or offences by one or more of the parties to the agreement if the agreement is carried out in accordance with their intentions, he is guilty of conspiracy . . ."

The purported action must "necessarily" involve the commission of a crime. Thus D^1 and D^2 must intend the illegal consequence. If, therefore, they agree that D^3 will seriously injure P, and, as a result, P dies, the conspiracy is not a conspiracy to murder, only to inflict g.b.h. (Quare whether this could include consequences that, though unforeseen, will necessarily follow, *e.g.* D^1 and D^2 agree to injure P, who has a thin skull and must die if injured even slightly? It is submitted that though this will "necessarily" follow, D^1 and D^2 are not guilty of conspiracy to murder as they do not foresee this result.)

> Section 1 (2): "Where liability for any offence may be incurred without knowledge on the part of the person committing it of any particular fact or circumstance necessary for the commission of the offence, a person shall nevertheless not be guilty of conspiracy . . . unless he and at least one other party to the agreement *intend or know* that that fact or circumstance shall or will exist . . ."

This adopts the common law as laid down in *Churchill* v. *Walton* (1967) that an agreement to commit a crime of strict liability must itself be made with knowledge of the facts that need not be shown on a charge of the principal offence. Thus D is guilty of abducting a minor even though he believes her to be 16 (*R.* v. *Prince, supra*) if she is, in fact only 15. D^1 and D^2 are only guilty of conspiracy to so abduct if they *know* that she is under 16.

What if D¹ and D² agree to commit a crime on certain conditions?

The problem here concerns the conduct "necessarily" involving commission of a crime. It seems reasonable that if D¹ and D² agree to ask P for a loan, but steal the money if he refuses, this is not a conspiracy to steal. The agreement can be successfully carried out without a crime *necessarily* being committed.

Where, however, D¹ and D² agree to steal from P provided he is not very big, a successful completion of this agreement does *necessarily* involve commission of a crime, and thus the agreement should constitute an indictable conspiracy.

Conspiracy to Defraud

This is made wider than is fraud under the *Theft Act*. It was described in *R.* v. *Sinclair* (1968) as:

> "To act with deliberate dishonesty to the prejudice of another person's rights."

In *Scott* v. *M.P.C.* (1974), the defendants conspired to produce copies of films without permission. The House of Lords in upholding the convictions stated firstly that deception is *not* a necessity here, and secondly:

> "It is clearly the law that an agreement by two or more by dishonesty to deprive a person of something which is his or to which he might be entitled . . . or injure some proprietary right of his, suffices to constitute the offence of conspiracy to defraud." (Vct. Dilhorne.)

In *R.* v. *Allsop* (1976), D arranged Hire Purchase agreements by making false representations to the finance companies. He claimed that he did not intend to cause any loss. The jury were directed to convict if they thought that D intended to prejudice P in an economic sense, though not necessarily in money. D's conviction was upheld.

Conspiracy and Morality

The House of Lords held in *Shaw* v. *D.P.P.* (1961) that it is an indictable conspiracy to corrupt public morals. Here, D agreed

to publish the "Ladies Directory" containing a list of prostitutes
and indications as to their services. *Shaw* was followed in *Knul-
ler* v. *D.P.P.* (1972). The defendants published a magazine
containing advertisements from homosexuals seeking partners.
Despite the fact that homosexual acts in private between consenting adults had been legalised in 1967, the convictions were
upheld by the House of Lords.

Their Lordships also held, by a majority, that the defendants
had committed the offence of "conspiracy to outrage public
decency." This common law offence is also preserved by the
1977 Act. The "outrage" must, it is thought, be as a result of
rather strong material.

Parties

As regards *statutory compromise*, the 1977 Act states:
> "2–(1) A person shall not . . . be guilty of conspiracy to
>   commit any offence if he is an intended victim of
>   that offence.
>   (2) A person shall not ... be guilty ... if the only
>   other person or persons with whom he agrees
>   are ...
>   (a) his spouse;
>   (b) a person under that the age of criminal
>   responsbility; and
>   (c) an intended victim ..."

It may be that section 5 (1) does not reflect the common law
position. In *R.* v. *Whitchurch* (1890), D was convicted of con-
spiring to procure her own abortion. Though this may theoreti-
cally still represent the common law, the definition is unlikely
ever to trouble the courts: D is unlikely to conspire to defraud
himself.

*What if D¹ and D² are charged with conspiracy, and only D¹
convicted?*

The answer lies in section 5 (8) which covers both statutory and common law conspiracies:

> "5–(8) *The fact that the person* or *persons who*, so far as appears from the indictment on which any person has been convicted of conspiracy, *were the only other parties to the agreement* on which his conviction was based *have been acquitted of conspiracy* by reference to that agreement . . . *shall not be a ground for quashing his conviction* unless under all the circumstances of the case his conviction is inconsistent with the acquittal of the other person or persons in question."

This gives statutory force to *R.* v. *Shannon* (1974). Thus where D^1 is acquitted and D^2 convicted of conspiracy, the result is not necessarily wrong. There may have been evidence that D^2 conspired with an unknown conspirator. Even if D^1 and D^2 were the sole conspirators, there may have been evidence admissible at the trial against D^2 but not against D^1. It must be stressed, however, that where the evidence is essentially the same against two defendants, any appeal court is likely to view the conviction of only one with scepticism.

Conspiring to do the Impossible

Common Law

Where the defendants agree to pursue a course of action which, when carried out, will not result in a crime's having been committed, there is no conspiracy. This follows from *D.P.P.* v. *Nock* (1978). The accused agreed to produce cocaine from powder they possessed, which would have been an offence under the *Misuse of Drugs Act*. Unknown to them, the powder was incapable of producing this substance. Their convictions were quashed by the House of Lords. Thus, conspiracy follows the reasoning of *Haughton* v. *Smith* as regards attempts. Nock is, of course, a case of "physical" impossibility.

Note that, on the facts of this case, the law is now governed by the 1977 Act, however *Nock* applies to the remaining common law conspiracies.

N.B. Here the defendants agreed to do a precise act, which could not have produced a criminal result. It would be different if they, *e.g.* decided to commit bank robberies, and the first bank they were to attack closed before it could be robbed.

The fact that D^1 and D^2 ultimately fail in their plan will not always cancel their liability for conspiracy. Thus Smith would have been guilty of conspiracy to handle the stolen tins (Quare if this is now conspiracy to defraud?)

Statutory Conspiracy

Note that under section 1 (1) the conduct must "necessarily amount to or involve the commission of an offence." One can use an analogy from *Nock*, where D^1 and D^2 are not liable as "it is not possible to achieve their object by the course of conduct agreed on."

Pushed to its logical conclusion, this would mean that the limits of conspiracy would be narrowed appreciably. Though it might be argued that section 1 (1) allows us to judge the accused from the consequences that they intended would follow, there is undoubtedly some limit where they have agreed on a course which cannot possibly produce that result. This limit is, at the moment, unclear.

CHAPTER 4

HOMICIDE

Homicide is the killing of another. If it is unlawful, then it may constitute murder, manslaughter or infanticide. The distinction between murder and manslaughter depends upon the accused's state of mind, thus there is really only the *actus reus* of homicide, these two offences differing in mens rea.

Whichever type of homicide be charged, it must be proved that the accused caused the death. There is an irrebuttable presumption that if death does not occur within a year and a day, the accused is not guilty of murder, but only of an offence under the *O.A.P. Act*, usually g.b.h. The year and a day rule also applies to manslaughter, *R.* v. *Dyson* (1908). The Crown must show that the accused hastened the death of the victim, even if only by one day, which creates problems concerning, *e.g.* the doctor who, through the use of drugs to save a terminal patient from agony, inevitably shortens his life.

Whether or not an intervening event can be said to cause the death is primarily a question of law. Obviously, if D mortally wounds P and P is killed one moment later by lightning, D will only be guilty of attempted murder at most. Where, however, the intervening cause is consequential on the defendant's attack, the courts are very loath to excuse him; see *R.* v. *Smith*, *R.* v. *Blaue* (*supra*).

It seems that D will also be guilty where the fear he deliberately creates in another causes their death. Thus in *R.* v. *Hayward* (1908), D was convicted of manslaughter when he chased his wife in a violent and threatening way, and she fell dead because of the shock to her heart.

Note that homicide by a British citizen anywhere in the world is indictable here.

(a) Murder

Mens Rea

This is known as "malice aforethought," which is purely a term of art. This necessarily includes an element of "specific intent."

Thus the Crown has three hurdles on a charge of murder.

They must show, *e.g.*:

    (1) That D hit P over the head, and that this assault caused P's death;

    (2) That the accused had the relevant mens rea in relation to this blow, *i.e.* he intended to hit P over the head;

    (3) That he had the requisite specific intent, *i.e.* he intended certain consequences to flow from this assault.

The specific intent of murder is itself divided into three categories.

  (i) D will be guilty if by his blow he *intends to kill P*.

  (ii) What if D *intends only to cause g.b.h.*?

In *R.* v. *Vickers* (1957), the defence argued that the Homicide Act overruled the so-called doctrine of "implied malice," whereby D is liable if he intends merely g.b.h. Here D viciously assaulted an old lady, who died as a result. Lord Goddard C.J. rejected the defence argument, though his judgment seems to be based on the assumption that a defendant intending g.b.h. is necessarily reckless as to the possibility of causing death. (Is this always so?) This doctrine is upheld by *Hyam*.

(iii) Is there a third head of specific intent?

D.P.P. v. *Smith* (1961). D, while carrying stolen goods in the boot of his car, was stopped by a policeman. To avoid capture he accelerated away. The officer hung onto the car bonnet but was thrown off when D swerved. He fell into the path of an oncoming vehicle and was killed. D maintained that he did not intend to cause the officer any serious harm, but Donovan J. directed the jury that if they thought a reasonable man would have foreseen such harm, D was guilty. The conviction was quashed by the Court of Appeal, but restored by the House of Lords. Thus an objective test became the rule in relation to the specific intent of murder. There are two ways of interpreting the rule in *Smith*, one is a purely *evidential* rule, the other as a rule of *substantive law*, and thus a third head of the specific intent of murder.

(a) If *Smith* lays down a rule of evidence, then it concerns how to prove what D intended or foresaw. The Crown, on a murder charge, must still prove that D intended death or g.b.h., but they can prove that such was his intention merely by showing that it was the "natural and probable" result of his actions. If this interpretation is correct, this rule of evidence (and it undoubtedly was the rule earlier this century) would apply to all crimes requiring proof of intention.

(b) If *Smith* is a legal rule then it adds a third head of specific intent. Thus D is guilty if he (i) intends to kill, (ii) intends g.b.h., (iii) does an act aimed at someone of which the natural and probable result is death or g.b.h. For the third head then, proof of intention is unnecessary.

As a result of protest at this decision, Parliament introduced section 8 of the *Criminal Justice Act* (*supra*). It will be remembered that section 8 lays down the rule that when proof of the accused's intention is required, it is not sufficient to look at the natural and probable results of his actions. Instead, the jury must decide what he actually thought. Thus if *Smith* had laid down a rule of evidence, this would have been overruled by section 8. This position was accepted in *R*. v. *Wallet* (1968). It is now certain that this case is incorrect, and *Smith* did lay down a legal rule, *i.e.* a "t ird head."

Hyam v. *D.P.P.* (1974)

In order to frighten her lover's new mistress, (B), D poured petrol through B's letter-box and set fire to it. The resultant fire caused the death of two children in the house. D maintained that her only intention was to frighten B, and not to harm her physically. On the way to B's house, however, she had checked to make sure that her lover was not in B's house so, she admitted, that he would come to no harm.

By a three to two majority the House of Lords upheld the conviction of murder. Lord Hailsham firstly rejected the argument that *Vickers* was wrong and secondly, declared that section 8 had not overruled *Smith*. Though his Lordship refused himself to overrule *Smith*, he re-drafted the specific intent of murder. Firstly he notes that for each head, the defendant's act must be "aimed at someone," and then the Crown must show that D had one of the following intents:

"(i) The intention to cause death.

 (ii) The intention to cause g.b.h. ... [as explained in *Smith* to mean really serious bodily injury] ...

(iii) [a] Where the defendant knows that there is a serious risk that death or g.b.h. will ensue from his acts ..., the intention to expose a potential victim to that risk ... (it does not matter that the act and the intention were aimed at a potential victim other than the one who succumbed).

[b] ... Without an intention of one of these three types the mere fact that the defendant's conduct is done in the knowledge that g.b.h. is likely or highly likely ... is not enough by itself to convert a homicide into murder."

1. Thus the "third head" is really one of recklessness, *i.e.* intentionally taking a risk.

2. There are still difficulties in distinguishing what will and will not be murder. *E.g.* D realises that serious injury is highly likely from his actions, yet goes on to commit them. He is, seemingly, within the exception [b] and this is not enough to convict, yet how can D say that he does not intend to expose the victim to this risk, even if only by "oblique" intent?

3. If there is a difference between [a] and [b], into which category would you put Mrs. Hyam? If the only difference is that in the former, the act must be "aimed at someone," how can one intend to expose a victim to harm by one's actions if those actions are *not* aimed at someone?

4. Students must read all the speeches in *Hyam*. Note particularly that Lord Hailsham's definition of "intention" includes elements of recklessness.

(b) Manslaughter

Manslaughter consists of two broad groups; cases where the accused has the *mens rea* for murder but, for some reason, his guilt is lessened (voluntary manslaughter), and cases where the accused has no "malice aforethought."

Voluntary Manslaughter
  (a) Provocation: If D is provoked into killing P then he is entitled to be convicted of manslaughter rather than murder. The common law definition encapsulated in the judgment of Devlin J. in *R. v. Duffy* (1949) stated that provocation was:
  ". . . some act or series of acts done by the dead man to the accused, which would cause in a reasonable person and actually causes in the accused, a sudden and temporary loss of self-control, rendering the accused so subject to passion as to make him . . . not master of his mind."
Thus the test was both objective (would a reasonable man have been so provoked?) and subjective (was the accused actually provoked?). The question of whether the reasonable man would have been provoked was a legal test, and the courts constructed a picture of this creature, who was neither pregnant (*R. v. Smith* (1914)) nor impotent (*Bedder* v. *D.P.P.* (1954)). The law was reformed by *Homicide Act 1957*, s. 3:
  "Where on a charge of murder there is evidence on which the jury can find that the person charged was provoked (whether by things done or by things said or by both together) to lose his self-control, the question whether the provocation was enough to make a reasonable man do as he did shall be left to be determined by the jury; and in determining that question the jury shall take into account everything both done and said according to the effect which, in their opinion, it would have on a reasonable man."

Thus the requirement that the provocation must come solely from the victim is abolished (see *R.* v. *Davies* (1975)) and it is made clear that provocation may be justified as a reaction to words alone. It is also clear that the judge can no longer lay down the qualities of the reasonable man, however, section 3 requires *some* evidence of provocation before the question is left to the jury, thus if the judge is of the opinion that there is no evidence that a reasonable man would have been provoked, may he withdraw the issue from the jury? It has been uncertain how far section 3 actually goes. Did the objective element still adopt the test of a hypothetical reasonable man "outside" the accused, or was one to consider whether the accused, with his characteristics, had behaved reasonably? These questions are partly answered by:

D.P.P. v. *Camplin* (1978)

D, who claimed that he was buggered and then insulted by P, killed him. The trial judge directed the jury that the consideration of the effect of this on the reasonable man required them to consider a reasonable adult, thus the fact that D was only 15 was irrelevant. The Court of Appeal allowed D's appeal, and the House of Lords affirmed this. Their Lordships make it quite clear the section 3 requires the jury to assume that:

> ". . . the reasonable man referred to in the question is a person having the power of self control to be expected of an ordinary person of the sex and age of the accused, but in other respects sharing such of the accused's characteristics as they think would affect the gravity of the provocation to him . . ." (*per* Lord Diplock).

His Lordship also makes it clear that, provided that there is some evidence that the accused was provoked, the judge must leave the question of whether a reasonable man would have been so provoked to the jury. Thus such cases as *Mancini* v. *D.P.P.* (1942) are no longer law.

Provocation must be left to the jury where D satisfies the evidential burden of showing that he was provoked. The jury must then consider:

1. Did D in fact lose his self control?
2. Would a reasonable (*i.e.* normally tempered) person in D's situation have lost his control?
3. Would a reasonable person have reacted as D did?

The jury must answer all three questions affirmatively to find provocation made out, though, naturally, the burden of proof that there was *not* provocation remains on the prosecution.

[*N.B.* This does not mean that in all cases concerning negligence, the court will adopt a similar test of the "reasonable man." Whether that test concerns the accused himself behaving reasonably, or a hypothetical reasonable man, is uncertain; possibly still the latter, though note *R.* v. *Hudson*, 1965]

If D makes a *mistake* as to facts which, had they been true would have permitted him to plead provocation, he may have the facts he honestly supposed to be true treated as though they were so. Thus in *R.* v. *Brown* (1776), where D killed P whom he mistakenly believed to be attacking him, he was allowed to plead provocation. Here D's mistake seems to have been reasonable (quare if it had not been, *infra,* "Mistake under Defences").

Drunkenness may affect provocation in one of two ways. First, it may make D lose his self control more easily. It is clear from *Camplin* that the normal-tempered reasonable man is not drunk; thus, though the jury must no doubt consider the defence, D is unlikely to succeed. It might be thought that, murder being a crime of specific intent, D will only be convicted of manslaughter anyway (*infra*), however, there may be instances where, though D has been drinking heavily, he is still aware of what he is doing.

In *R.* v. *Letennock* (1917), however, D's appeal was allowed where his drunkenness did not lessen his degree of self control, but was responsible for his making a mistake more easily, *i.e.* he believed that he was being attacked. It may be that after *Majewski* v. *D.P.P.* (*infra*), D's drunkenness will not be allowed to excuse him:

If D is mistaken, the test is:

1. Did D honestly believe a set of facts [his mistaken belief, (quare if this must be a reasonable mistake)]?
2. Did he lose his self-control as a result?
3. Would a reasonable man, supposing these facts to have been true, have lost his control and retaliated as D did because of the situation created by those facts?

(b) Diminished responsibility: This defence, which again reduces murder to manslaughter, was introduced by the *Homicide Act 1957*, s. 2:

"Where a person kills or is party to the killing of another, he shall not be convicted of murder if he was *suffering from such abnormality of mind* (whether arising from a condition of arrested or retarded development of mind or any inherent causes or induced by disease or injury) *as substantially impairs his mental responsibility* for his acts and omissions in doing or being party to the killing."

Note the relationship with the defence of insanity (*infra*). Due to the rigidity of the McNaghten rules, the majority of cases where D suffers from some mental aberration are now pleaded under section 2. The burden of proof is on the defence, on the balance of probabilities.

In *R.* v. *Spriggs* (1958), the trial judge left the jury to decide whether or not D came within section 2, with no explanation of its legal effect. Though this seems to be a case of allowing a jury to interpret a statute, the Court of Appeal held that this was correct.

In *R.* v. *Byrne* (1960), however, the judge told the jury that the accused's inability to control his actions could not bring him within section 2. D strangled a young woman because of inordinate sexual urges, which he found impossible to control. The Court of Appeal held this direction wrong. It was for the jury to decide whether or not D's conduct indicated an "abnormality of mind." The judge, however, must give the jury some explanation of the effect of section 2 (*R.* v. *Terry*). The role of the jury is neatly summed up by Lord Keith in *Walton* v. *The Queen*:

> ". . . on an issue of diminished responsibility the jury are entitled and indeed bound to consider not only the medical evidence but the evidence on the whole facts and circumstances of the case. These include the nature of the killing, the conduct of the accused before, at the time of and after it and any history of mental abnormality. It being recognised that the jury on occasion may properly refuse to accept medical evidence . . . what the jury are essentially seeking to ascertain is whether at the time of the killing the accused was suffering from a state of mind bordering on but not amounting to insanity. That task is to be approached in a broad common sense way."

Thus these cases are more than usually dependant on the facts of each case, and the jury's view of those facts.

Involuntary Manslaughter

This is the unlawful killing of another without "malice aforethought."

N.B. Always take care to tell an examiner which type of involuntary manslaughter you are considering, *e.g.* "this problem concerns liability for manslaughter by gross negligence." If a problem concerns more than one type, consider each separately.

(a) Manslaughter under the "Unlawful Act Doctrine": This is constructive manslaughter. D is guilty if he *intends* to perform an act which is illegal, although he is only grossly negligent in relation to causing any personal injury.

In *D.P.P.* v. *Newbury* (1976), D threw a paving stone from a railway bridge onto the track as a train was approaching. The stone hit and killed the guard. D's conviction for manslaughter was upheld by the House of Lords. It had been argued, following a dictum of Lord Denning, that the accused must foresee the risk of injury, but this was rejected.

"In judging whether the act was dangerous, the test is not did the accused recognise that it was dangerous but would all sober and reasonable people recognise its danger." (Lord Salmon.)

Thus D must commit an unlawful act which is objectively dangerous.

It has been held that "unlawful" encompasses more than merely the criminal. In *R.* v. *Fenton* (1830) D committed a tort (trespass) by throwing stones into a mine, causing death. The act must of course be dangerous, and on the facts of *Fenton* itself, D would also be guilty of committing a criminally unlawful act, probably Criminal Damage.

It seems that one must distinguish between an act which is unlawful in itself, *e.g.* assault, and a lawful activity which becomes unlawful because of the manner in which it is performed, *e.g.* Careless Driving. The former may constitute the "unlawful act," the latter may not. This follows from *Andrews* v. *D.P.P.* (1937).

In *R.* v. *Lamb* (1967) there was held to be no unlawful act when D pointed a gun in jest at P, the gun going off and killing P. D did not appreciate that the gun might fire, and had no intention of frightening P. As he also knew that P was not afraid, there was no assault, and thus no unlawful act.

In *R.* v. *Larkin* (1943) D threatened P with a knife. P being groggy with drink fell against it and was killed. D was held guilty as his unlawful act (assault) was likely to injure someone.

Unlawful Omissions: In R. Senior (1899) D neglected a child in contravention of the predecessor to the *1933 Children and Young Persons Act*, and was held guilty of manslaughter as this lack of care resulted in the child's death.

In *R.* v. *Lowe* (1973), however, the defendant's conviction for manslaughter was quashed by the Court of Appeal. D who was slow-witted, so neglected his child that it died from dehydration and emaciation. His conviction for wilful neglect under the 1933 Act was upheld. The manslaughter count was quashed, as the Court interpreted *Andrews* to have laid down a rule excluding cases of "manslaughter by neglect" from this head. It is submitted that this is not in fact the same as Lord Atkin's description of "a lawful act performed unlawfully." The omission to care for the child was, because of the 1933 Act, an unlawful omission, and as the Act requires "wilfulness" that omission was presumably intended. It is not, it will be remembered, necessary to prove that D foresaw or intended the result. *Lowe* may be interpreted as laying down a stricter test for unlawful omission than for acts, though no such point is made in the later House of Lords case of *Newbury*.

(b) Manslaughter committed due to gross negligence: It is not enough that D caused death by his carelessness, even if this would have rendered him liable in tort.

In *R.* v. *Finney* (1874) D was held not to be guilty of manslaughter when after telling a lunatic to get out of the bath, his attention having been attracted elsewhere, he put his hand on the wrong tap and poured scalding water, instead of cold, over P. To define exactly what conduct this head embraces is impossible. Lord Hewart C.J. noted in *R.* v. *Bateman* (1925):

> "In explaining to juries the test which they should apply to determine whether the negligence . . . amounted or did not amount to a crime, judges have used many epithets, such as 'culpable,' 'criminal,' 'gross,' 'wicked' . . . but whatever epithet be used . . . in order to establish criminal liability the facts must be such that in the opinion of the jury the negligence of the accused went beyond a mere matter of compensation between subjects and showed such disregard for the life and safety of others as to amount to a crime against the state and conduct deserving of punishment."

Lord Hewart considers the word "reckless" to be the most appropriate, however, he does not mean to use the word in the sense it is generally used today, but rather means an "objective recklessness"; otherwise "gross negligence."

The court in *Lamb* considered that, had the jury been so directed, they might well have convicted D if they:

"... considered his view as to their being no danger was formed in a criminally negligent way."

D may be liable here for *omission* to perform an act where he was under a duty even if only by contract, to perform that act. Thus in *P*. v. *Pitwood* (*supra*) D was held guilty when he failed to do his job of opening the level crossing gates before the arrival of a train, this resulting in an accident. In *R*. v. *Stone and Dobinson* (1977) the defendants were found guilty of manslaughter by gross neglect when they failed to look after the welfare of P, an invalid who was living with them and helping them financially, a duty to care for P's welfare having been cast upon the accused. If a question involves an unlawful act and thus requires consideration of (a) above, it may also require consideration under this head. *E.g.* in *Andrews,* though the House of Lords rejected the unlawful act doctrine, they upheld D's conviction on the ground that he was criminally negligent.

It has been suggested that there is a third head of involuntary manslaughter based upon *R*. v. *Pike* (1961). Here, D administered a dangerous chemical to P in order to increase sexual satisfaction. Though he had used the substance before without harmful effect, on this occasion it caused P's death. The Court of Appeal upheld a direction that D was guilty if he knew that exposure to the substance would expose P to the risk of some harm, and recklessly caused her to inhale it. It is not certain as to what consequences the "recklessness" refers to. If death or g.b.h., then this seems to come very close to murder (see *Hyam*, *infra*). It is thought that if D's *mens rea* is anything less, it is far better to consider the two established forms of involuntary manslaughter.

(c) Infanticide

A conviction here reduces what would otherwise be murder, leaving the court with the same discretion as would a verdict of manslaughter. *The Infanticide Act 1938* s. 1 (1) states:

> "Where a woman by any wilful act or omission causes the death of a child being a child under the age of twelve months, but at the time of the act or omissions the balance of her mind was disturbed by reason of her not having fully recovered from the effect of giving birth . . . or by reason of the effect of lactation consequent upon the birth of the child . . . notwithstanding . . . the offence would have amounted to murder, she shall be guilty of . . . infanticide . . ."

(i) The Act thus does not apply if the mother kills another child other than the one under 12 months.

(ii) If, on a charge of murder, the accused pleads guilty to infanticide, she must raise some evidence (the "evidential burden") of this. The burden of proving murder still rests with the Crown.

(iii) Note the relationship with the defences of insanity and diminished responsibility.

(d) Offences concerning Suicide

Under the *Suicide Act 1961*, suicide ceases to be a crime for the principal offender. Liability is possible, however, if at least two people are involved. This may be under the *Suicide Act* itself, or under the *1957 Homicide Act*. By section 2 of the *Suicide Act:*

> "A person who aids, abets, counsels or procures the suicide of another or an attempt by another to commit suicide shall be liable . . ."

As usual, motive is irrelevant. Thus the procuring of a poison in order to cut short an agonising death is as much an offence as counselling an elderly relative to "end it all" in order to inherit his money. The consent of the D.P.P. is needed before this indictment may be laid. By *Homicide Act* s. 4 (1):

"It shall be manslaughter and shall not be murder for a person acting in pursuance of a suicide pact between him and another to kill the other or be a party to the other being killed by a third person;"

and by section 4 (3):

"[A suicide pact is] a common agreement between two or more persons having for its object the death of all of them, whether or not each is to take his own life, but nothing done by a person who enters into a suicide pact shall be treated as [such] . . . unless it is done while he has the settled intention of dying in pursuance of it."

(i) If the accused is charged with murder, the onus of proving a suicide pact is upon him, presumably on the balance of probabilities.

(ii) Killing in the course of a suicide pact is an offence under the *Homicide Act* and NOT the *Suicide Act*. Causing death in this way is thus manslaughter.

(iii) Complicity in another's suicide under section 2 of the *Suicide Act* may only be charged where the victim kills himself. Thus if, on this charge, it is shown that D killed the victim, D is not guilty under section 2.

CHAPTER 5

OFFENCES AGAINST THE PERSON ACT 1861

1. Assaults

We are concerned with 4 types, which are, in order of gravity: "Common Assault"; assault occasioning actual bodily harm;

wounding or inflicting grievous bodily harm; wounding or causing grievous bodily harm with intent.

(i) Assault and battery

An assault is an action by D intended to make P fear immediate personal violence. A battery is an unlawful striking of P by D. In practice, the term, "assault" is used to cover both, and "Common Assault" is an offence under *O.A.P.A.* s. 47.

A knowledge of the tort of assault is useful. D will be guilty of assault even though he is unable to carry out a battery, *e.g.* D points an unloaded gun at P, but P thinks, as D intended him to, that it is loaded.

There is dicta in old cases (*e.g. R.* v. *Meade* (1823)) that words alone cannot constitute an assault, though this may not be true where D has placed P in an obviously threatening situation. Thus Lord Goddard C.J. was of the opinion that a thief shouting "get out the knives" would amount to an assault (*R.* v. *Wilson* (1955)).

Attention is often paid to *Tuberville* v. *Savage* (1660), where D made to pull out his sword, but was acquitted as he had declared that he would not stab P because it was Assize time. The principle from this case must not be pushed too far. It can hardly apply where D, a large man standing threateningly over P brandishing an implement, uses words to indicate that he will not, in fact, strike P. Any reasonable man might be afraid of harm in such a situation.

Obviously D is guilty if he intends the assault. It follows from *R.* v. *Venna* (1975) that D will be guilty where he is reckless.

For battery, the force need not be applied directly as in *Scott* v. *Shepherd* (1773) where D threw a lighted squib into a crowd resulting in its being thrown in panic, ultimately injuring P. D was held liable in tort, and this decision would seem also to be applicable to the criminal law.

An assault is necessarily carried out without the victim's

consent. If that consent is obtained by fraud, it seems that one must distinguish fraud going to the nature of the act from fraud merely in relation to the circumstances. Thus in *R.* v. *Williams* (1933), where D pretended that intercourse was a method of improving the voice, there would seem to be an assault. In *R.* v. *Clarence* (1888), however, there was no assault where P consented to intercourse with D, although D failed to tell her that he was suffering from venereal disease.

Consent will not constitute a defence where P is too young to understand to what he is consenting, or where that consent is obtained by duress. It seems that the amount of pain one may consent to is limited. In *R.* v. *Donovan* (1934), D beat a 17-year-old girl with a cane, the girl apparently consenting. Though D's conviction was quashed, the Court of Appeal were of the opinion that consent would have been irrelevant had the jury found that the blows were struck with the intention of causing some harm. Moderate and reasonable force may be used by parents and teachers, but should the force be excessive, no motive, no matter how well-intentioned, will excuse it.

An assault may be an "aggravated one." Most important is assaulting a police officer. By *Police Act 1964,* s. 51:

"1. Any person who assaults a constable in the execution of his duty, or a person assisting a constable in the execution of his duty, shall be guilty of an offence . . .

3. Any person who resists or wilfully obstructs a constable in the execution of his duty, or a person assisting a constable in the execution of his duty, shall be guilty of an offence . . ."

(i) A constable would seem to be in the execution of his duty if his conduct falls within the general scope of preventing crime and catching offenders—*R.* v. *Winterfield* (1964).

(ii) It does not seem to matter whether or not D realises that P is a constable (*Forbes* v. *Webb*, 1865), thus the only *mens rea* necessary is that of simple assault. The effect of this can be seen in *McBride* v. *Turnock* (1964), where D aimed a blow at X, missed, and hit P, who was a constable. Though D was obviously guilty of assault via the doctrine of transferred malice, he was also held liable under section 51 of the *Police Act* as he had caused the *actus reus* (hitting the P.C.) and had the requisite mens (of assault).

(iii) Section 51 covers any act of obstruction, including more than just physical obstruction. In *Betts* v. *Stevens* (1910), D was held guilty when he warned other drivers that they were approaching a speed trap. In *Hinchcliffe* v. *Sheldon* (1955), Lord Goddard C.J. defined obstructing as ". . . making it more difficult for the police to carry out their duties."

(ii) Assault Occasioning Actual Bodily Harm

This is covered by section 47 of the 1861 Act. Presumably, by implication from *Hyam*, the harm here is something less than really serious. Though the *actus reus* requires proof of some physical injury, the mens rea is simply that of assault. The test of causation is satisfied when the harm is the natural consequence of the assault. Thus in *R.* v. *Roberts* (1971), D threatened to sexually assault P, with the result that she jumped out of D's car and was injured. D was convicted. It would seem, however, that where the victim's reaction is wholly unreasonable, the chain of causation might be said to have been broken.

(iii) Wounding or Inflicting G.B.H.

By section 20 of the 1861 Act:

> "Whosoever shall unlawfully and maliciously wound or inflict any grievous bodily harm upon any other person, either with or without any weapon or instrument shall be guilty . . ."

As noted, this requires some serious injury. The "wounding" refers to an actual breaking of the skin, and not just bruising.

It does not seem to be necessary that the assault be directly inflicted. In *R.* v. *Martin* (1881), D put out the lights of a theatre and placed an iron bar across the exit, causing serious injury to a number of people. D was convicted of inflicting g.b.h., despite the fact that "inflicting" seems to indicate a direct assault. (Section 18, but not section 20, contains the words "by any means whatsoever.") In *R.* v. *Halliday* (1889), D so terrified his wife that she jumped out of a window and was injured. D was found guilty of "inflicting" as his putting her in such fear caused her to jump.

Note that *Clarence* (*supra*) was acquitted under section 20, but the court placed strong emphasis on the fact that P was his wife.

The *mens rea* for section 20 is obviously less than intent to cause the consequential injury, otherwise the conviction would be under section 18. According to *R.* v. *Mowatt* (1968);

> ". . . the word 'maliciously' does impart upon the part of the person who unlawfully inflicts the wound, or other grievous bodily harm an awareness that his act may have the consequence of causing *some physical harm* . . . It is quite unnecessary that the accused should have foreseen that his unlawful act might cause physical harm of the gravity described in the section . . ."

Mowatt has been criticised, especially since the court seems to have taken an objective view as to proof of D's intention (now see section 8, *C.J.A.*, *supra*). It is difficult, however, to see how a court can require a much stricter test for the *mens rea*, without overlapping section 18.

(iv) Wounding or Causing G.B.H. with Intent

Section 18 of the *O.A.P.A.* states:

> "Whosoever shall unlawfully and maliciously by any means whatsoever wound or cause grievous bodily harm to any person with intent to do some grievous bodily harm to any person or with intent to resist or prevent the lawful apprehension or detainer of any person, shall be guilty . . ."

This is a crime of *specific intent*. The Crown must show:

  (i) D performed an act which caused really serious bodily injury to another;

 (ii) D intended to bring about that act, either in relation to P or another;

(iii) D either (a) intended that that act would have as its consequence the causing of really serious injury, or (b) intended that by that act he would be able to escape or resist arrest, or help another in so doing.

Section 18 uses the word "cause" rather than "inflict." It may be that because of this, it is sufficiently wide enough to cover cases like *Clarence*, however, the prosecution would have to show that D intended the serious injury.

As section 18 requires intent to cause g.b.h. there seems little point in the term "maliciously" being employed here. One possible explanation is that it necessitates proof of foresight of harm when the accused is charged with intent to escape. (But see *Mowatt* where the judges state that the term adds nothing in section 18).

If there were no section 18, what would be the *mens rea* of section 20? Would it, then, be a crime of specific intent?

(v) Administering Poison

Sections 23 and 24 of the 1861 Act make it an offence to administer a poison or destructive or noxious thing to another.

Like section 18, section 24 requires the Crown to prove that the accused intended to cause g.b.h. (or endanger that other's life). Thus, section 23 creates an offence that can be committed recklessly (*R*. v. *Cunningham* (1957)), but the prosecution must show that the substance actually caused serious harm, or endangered life.

"Noxious thing" was held in *R*. v. *Cato* (1976) to include heroin.

CHAPTER 6

THE THEFT ACT (1)

The offences outlined in the *1968 Theft Act* were mostly covered by the 1861 and *1916 Larceny Acts,* which themselves were merely consolidation statutes. The *Theft Act* sweeps away these statutes, and much of the old case law, the latter being useful only as a guideline of how the courts might interpret the new act.

Students must be familiar with the relevant sections, so that they know, *e.g.* what are the ulterior offences necessary for a conviction of burglary under section 9 (1) (*a*). Care must be taken to spot questions involving the inter-relation of sections, thus D's action of trespassing and taking while brandishing an implement may involve a discussion of theft, burglary, robbery and possibly blackmail.

Theft

Section 1 states:

> "(1) A person is guilty of theft if he dishonestly appropriates property belonging to another with the intention of permanently depriving the other of it . . .
>
> (2) It is immaterial whether the appropriation is made with a view to gain or is made for the thief's own benefit."

Each of the requirements of section 1 is explained by one of the following five sections. *Note* that *theft is always committed under section 1 (1)*. A problem may mainly concern dishonesty, and thus require detailed consideration of section 2. It must NOT be stated, however, that "theft is committed under section 2 of the Theft Act." This annoys examiners intensely.

Actus Reus

This consists of "appropriating property belonging to

another." "Appropriation" is explained by section 3, and obviously goes much further than simply "taking and carrying away."

> "3–(1) Any *assumption* by a person *of the rights of an owner* amounts to an appropriation, and this includes, where he has come by the property (innocently or not) without stealing it, any *later assumption* of a right to it *by keeping or dealing with it as owner*."

Appropriation thus includes "assuming the rights of an owner." English law does not, however, contain a clear list of what constitute the "rights of an owner." It is no doubt the right of an owner to keep his silver locked away, throw away his rubbish, destroy his book and wash his car. No doubt any discussion of theft in the latter situation is prevented by the requirement of the intention to permanently deprive, but note the explanation of this aspect by section 6 (*infra*).

Where D comes by property innocently, he may still be guilty. Say that D finds an old coin in the street and believing it worthless and its owner untraceable, pockets it. At this moment he is not guilty of theft as he is not dishonest. Later, he learns that the coin is valuable but still decides to keep it. Now he is dishonest, however, the appropriation occurred sometime before. Section 3 (1) thus refers to a later appropriation, here, D's later decision, on finding out the coin's value, to keep it. One possible problem here is that D's later appropriation was purely mental, *i.e.* deciding to keep the coin. How, one might ask, can an element of the *actus reus* be mental? Of course, when D later touches the coin, *e.g.* to hide it at his home, the later appropriation is physical. If he is arrested before this stage, it might be argued that his omission to return the coin constitutes an *actus reus* (*supra*) as he is then under a duty to return the coin to its owner. The position is similar where D acquires possession as a baillee, and later decides to sell the baillor's goods.

Though there is academic argument to the contrary, the

courts seem to have rejected the view that D can be guilty
where he has a "conditonal intent" to steal, *e.g.* D examines the
property of P in order to see if it is worth stealing. In *R.* v.
Easom (1971), D picked up P's handbag, examined the contents and, on finding nothing worth taking, put it back. His
conviction was quashed by the Court of Appeal, Edmund
Davies L.J. stating:

> "What might loosely be described as a 'conditional'
> appropriation will not do. If the appropriator has it in mind
> merely to deprive the owner of such of his property as, on
> examination proves worth taking and then finding that the
> booty is to him valueless, leaves it ready to hand to be
> repossessed by the owner, he has not stolen."

Quare a conviction for attempt? (*supra*).

Appropriation and Consent

Perhaps the main difficulty here concerns the situation where
P consents to D's taking of his property. It is vital to bear in
mind two possible cases;

(i) D tricks P into allowing him to have possession of P's
property, *e.g.* D admires P's new watch and asks to
examine it, whereupon D runs away. There is never any
question of P's ownership of the property being in doubt.

(ii) D gains ownership of the property, *e.g.* D pays P for a
sofa-table with a cheque he knows to be worthless. The
resultant voidable contract is competent to pass the
property to D until the contract is avoided.

In both situations P consents to D's possession of the property
yet in (i), which denotes a situation of "larceny by a trick" under
the old law, there is no problem with a charge of theft. (ii)
however, is more appropriately dealt with by section 15 (*infra*).

In *R.* v. *Greenberg* (1972), D pulled up to a petrol pump and
filled the tank of his car, apparently intending to pay. As there
was a large queue, D drove off, D's actions could not constitute
theft as the ownership of the petrol had passed to him, as the

owner of the station intended it to. D has therefore made off without paying for what is now his.

In *R.* v. *Meech* (1974), D agreed to cash a cheque for X. While waiting for it to be cleared, D discovered that X had obtained the cheque illegally. Angry at this, D arranged with Y and Z to fake a robbery of the proceeds from the cheque. This they did though the police, who were called in order to add realism, discovered the truth. D was convicted of theft. It is important to note that the time of appropriation is not when the money is taken from the bank with a dishonest intention—presumably D is still acting in relation to the money in accord with permission given by X—but only when the fake robbery is staged, the latter constituting the actual (later) appropriation.

Where D obtains ownership of the property it is not enough to show that he has appropriated that property, the Crown must also show that the property belonged to another. Thus cases involving theft upon the transfer of ownership also require consideration of section 5 (*infra*). It must be noted that the appropriate charge here is for obtaining by deception (section 15) unfortunately, it is still necessary to consider theft also.

Lawrence v. *M.P.C.* (1972)

D, a taxi-driver, agreed to take P, a newly-arrived Italian student, a short distance. D pretended that the journey was long and expensive and, when P offered his wallet, D took £6. The correct fare should have been 52½p. D was charged not with obtaining by deception, but with theft. The immediate question in the House of Lords was whether D could be convicted even though the owner had consented to the taking. This their lordships held he could be. To have held otherwise would mean that "larceny by a trick" is not theft.

The case has wider implications. If D is guilty of theft when he obtains property by deception, is not section 15 then redundant? Dicta in the Court of Appeal suggests that this is so:

"... in any case where the facts would establish a charge under section 15 (1) they would also establish a charge under section 1 (1)" (Megaw L.J.).

This, however, must be doubted. It seems from the House of Lords that the overlap is not complete:

"... there are cases which only come within section 1 (1) and some which are only within section 15. If in this case the appellant had been charged under section 15 (1), he would, I expect, have contended that there was no deception ..." (Vct. Dilhorne).

Was there a deception?

As regards the ratio of *Lawrence* in the Lords, *i.e.* that the taking need not be without the consent of the owner, the decision is faultless. If one accepts dicta in the Court of Appeal, however (which was not specifically objected to in the Lords), then D will be guilty of theft where he obtains ownership of P's goods. This last point must be regarded as uncertain. In all cases where D obtains property, whether possession or ownership, by deception, always point out to the examiner first that the simplest and most appropriate charge is under section 15.

There is another reason why section 15 may be redundant, *infra.*, section 5 (4).

Appropriation by force

What if D obtains "consent" to his appropriation by forcing P to give it to him? If D merely threatens P saying "hand it over or else ..." theft has obviously been committed, so indeed has robbery. Slightly more difficult is the situation where D says "sell me your Sheraton chairs for £5 or else ..." Opinion is divided as to whether this creates a valid contract, which is merely voidable, or a completely void one. If the former, then D actually becomes the owner of the chairs for the time being. Nevertheless, it seems certain that D will still be guilty of theft. In the old case of *R.* v. *McGrath* (1869) P attended an auction but made no bid. D insisted that P had made a bid for some cloth, and would not allow P to leave until she paid, out of fright. D was convicted of larceny. The result would doubtless be the same today, particularly so in the light of the court's reluctance to explore complex civil law questions (see *R.* v. *Nordeng*).

Appropriation by "sale"

If D is in possession of P's property as bailee, and he sells it to X, he is obviously guilty of theft as this is a later appropriation by ". . . dealing with it as owner" (section 3 (1)).

More difficult is the position where D attempts to sell property of which he is not in possession. D "sells" P a car left on the road with its keys in, or "sells" a visiting tourist the Crown Jewels. Of use is the old case of *R.* v. *Bloxham* (1943). D showed P a refrigerator belonging to his employer, and pretended that it was his own. P paid D for it, but did no physical act in relation to it. He was acquitted of larceny of the fridge, as he was not a bailee, and had not attempted to remove it. It seems likely that this now constitutes "assuming the rights of an owner" and thus appropriation. Note, however, that the question of intending to permanently deprive still remains (*infra*). It has been argued that this situation, where D's primary objective is to obtain money from the would-be purchaser by deception, should still constitute theft of the article purportedly sold. Thus I would commit theft by "selling" the Coronation Coach to a tourist.

In *R.* v. *Pitham and Hehl* (1977) D was convicted of theft when he offered for sale furniture in P's house, knowing that P was in prison and unable to prevent him.

It may be that section 6 requires us to differentiate between the defendant who deceives X into buying Y's goods realising that X might well take them away, and the defendant who merely uses Y's property as an object for his fraud, with no prospect of X obtaining delivery. Thus the defendant in *Pitham* recognised what would happen to the furniture. It is not so where D sells the royal coach. D has obtained the tourist's money contrary to section 15, but there is no earthly chance of the latter collecting. Though D is assuming the rights of an owner, *i.e.* the right to sell, it is submitted that such a case is not properly theft, and there is certainly no intent to permanently deprive the Crown of the coach.

Section 3 (2) states:

> "Where property or a right or interest in property is or purports to be transferred for value to a person acting in good faith, no later assumption by him of rights which he believed himself to be acquiring shall, by reason of any defect in the transferor's title, amount to theft."

D buys a car from X in good faith. A week later he learns that the car was stolen, and therefore he has no legal right to it. He keeps it. Though this might have constituted a "later appropriation," section 3 (2) makes it clear that D is not guilty of theft. Note that D must have *bought* the property and in good faith.

N.B. D may be in trouble if he later sells the car. Section 3 (2) only protects him from liability for theft, thus if he sells the car to Z, presumably representing that Z will acquire title to it, D may be liable under section 15 for obtaining the price by deception.

Also, section 3 (2) does not exempt D from liability from handling, so that if he sells the car to X, who receives it knowing the truth (and is therefore guilty of handling), D has aided and abetted that handling.

"Property" is defined in s. 4:

> "(1) Property includes money and all other property, real or personal including things in action and other intangible property."

Thus, apparently, anything which may be "appropriated" can be stolen. "Things in action" would cover, *e.g.* theft of his overdraft by a dishonest bank clerk, via false entries in the accounts.

Generally, land cannot be stolen. Thus the dishonest neighbour who moves the fences so that his garden is enlarged at his neighbour's expense is not a thief. (But quare a conviction under section 15, or for conspiracy to defraud). Land may be stolen, however, where D:

(a) Is a trustee, or one authorised to sell (*e.g.* a solicitor or estate agent);

(b) is not in possession and appropriates by severing (*e.g.* D removes P's garden gate);

(c) is a tenant and appropriates the whole or part of a fixture.

This leaves several gaps. Thus, *e.g.* the licencee or squatter who appropriates a fixture, and the tenant who severs that which is not part of a fixture, do not commit theft.

D will not be guilty when, though not in possession of land, he "... *picks* mushrooms growing wild on any land or ... *picks* flowers, fruit or foliage from a plant growing *wild* on any land ... unless he does it for *reward* or for *sale* or *other commercial purpose*" (section 4 (3)).

1. Note "wild." D is guilty of theft if he picks mushrooms carefully cultivated by his neighbour.

2. Note "pick." D is presumably guilty if he uproots the whole plant.

3. "Reward" or "sale" might mean exchanging a few mushrooms for a pint in a pub. If, however, one reads "commercial purpose" to be essential, and "reward" and "sale" simply as examples of commercial purpose, then something much more planned is doubtless required.

N.B. This provision acquires an importance far in excess of its practical application, owing to a wholly unnatural obsession which, for some obscure reason, examiners seem to display in it.

Sections 4 (4) declares that wild creatures are to be considered property, except that they may only be stolen when not ordinarily kept in captivity if they have been reduced or are being reduced into possession by or on behalf of another, and the animal or carcase has not since been abandoned. Thus poaching is generally not theft, but where D steals a pheasant from a poacher, he does commit theft.

"*Belonging to another*" is explained by section 5:

"(1) Property shall be regarded as belonging to any person having *possession or control* of it, or having any property right or interest (not being an equitable interest arising only from an agreement to transfer or grant an interest)."

The victim of a theft needs therefore ownership, possession or control. Possession need not be lawful, thus it is theft where D steals from P, who has himself just stolen the property. The courts are very reluctant to say that any property has been abandoned so that no one is in possession or control of it. This can be seen in *R.* v. *Woodman* (1974). Company A owned a disused factory, and sold the right to take any scrap metal from it to company B. B took all the metal that they considered it economic to extract. Subsequently, the site became abandoned, though A's servants put up fences and keep-out notices, and checked the site once or twice a year. Two years later, D went onto the site and took the remaining scrap. He was convicted of theft from company A. Despite having sold all the metal on the site A were, for the purposes of the *Theft Act*, in control of the articles still on it.

What if D owns the property?

Where D is part-owner, he clearly steals from the other joint owners (*R.* v. *Bonner* (1970)).

Where D is the only owner, he cannot steal unless some other person has a legal right to exempt him from possession. Thus if D takes his radio to P, a repairer, P may keep the radio until P pays for the repairs. This is known as a "repairers lien." Should D take back the radio without paying, he commits theft.

In *R.* v. *Turner* (No. 2) (1971), D left his car at P's garage for repairs. Before the bill was paid, the car was stolen, and later discovered in D's possession. P undoubtedly did have a lien on the car, unfortunately, the trial judge told the jury to disregard any question of a lien and concentrated on D's obvious dishonesty. D was convicted. It is submitted that the reasoning here is faulty. D may have been dishonest, but theft requires an *actus reus*. A vital part of this is that the property should belong to another. If one disregards the lien, P had no right to keep the car, and thus D had every right to take back his own property. D can only be convicted if one does consider the lien. (See *R.* v. *Meredith* (1973).)

Again one must consider *Lawrence*. If D did become the owner of the notes, he did not steal property from another. It has been argued that P did not intend to pass ownership of anything in excess of the correct fare or that the money did belong to P just before D stole it. Neither explanation is particularly convincing.

In *R.* v. *Gilks* (1972), D was paid £106 instead of £10 as a result of a mistake by a betting-shop manager. D claimed, *inter alia*, that he had become the owner of the money and, thus, it did not belong to another. D was convicted of theft, and his appeal rejected by the Court of Appeal on the grounds that, due to the manager's mistake, the ownership of the extra money had not passed to D. This reasoning has been heavily criticised.

Two specific instances are made theft where P willingly passes ownership of the property to D.

(i) Section 5 (3) states:

"Where a person receives property from or an account of another, and is *under an obligation to retain* and deal with *that property* or proceeds in a particular way, *the property* or other proceeds *shall be regarded* (as against him) *as belonging to another*."

Section 5 (3) catches the milk roundsman who receives money from a housewife, which he is under an obligation to give to his boss, and spends it. Likewise where P gives D, a decorator, money for paint in order for him to decorate P's

house and D squanders it, D's conduct is covered by section 5
(3). Care must be taken not to push section 5 (3) too far,
however.

In *R.* v. *Hall* (1972), D, a travel agent, took clients' money on
the understanding that he would arrange trips abroad. The
money was paid into the firm's general trading account and, the
firm being in a hopeless financial position, no holidays material-
ised. D's conviction for theft was quashed by the Court of
Appeal. Despite the fact that D was under an obligation to *act*
in a certain way:

> ". . . what was not here established was that these clients
> expected D to 'retain and deal with *that property or its
> proceeds* in a particular way and that an 'obligation' to do
> so was undertaken by the appellant. We must make clear,
> however, that each case turns on its own facts." *Per*
> Edmund Davies L.J.

It will usually happen that D is not under an obligation to deal
with property or its proceeds in a certain way, but merely to
ensure that, at the appropriate time, he has sufficient funds to
perform the contract. If he fails to do so, he is not a thief. It is, in
such cases, for the jury to decide whether the property was in
fact so entrusted. (See *R.* v. *Hayes*, 1976.)

N.B. If the Crown had been able to show that D took the
money knowing that the holidays would not or might not take
place, D may have been liable under section 15.

(ii) Section 5 (4) states:

> "where a person gets property *by another's mistake* and is
> *under an obligation to make restoration* (in whole or in
> part) of the property or its proceeds . . . the property . . .
> shall be regarded (as against him) as belonging to the
> person entitled to restoration . . ."

Thus where P mistakenly gives D something to which D is not
entitled and he, realising P's mistake, keeps the property, his
conduct is covered by section 5 (4). The obligation must be a
legal, and not merely a moral, one. In the pre-Theft Act deci-

sion *Moynes* v. *Cooper* (1956), D was given an advance on his week's wages. At the end of the week, the clerk mistakenly paid D his full wage without a deduction for the advance. D, dishonestly, kept it. He could not be convicted of larceny. He could now be convicted of theft, because of section 5 (4).

Note that section 5 (4) applies only where the *ownership passes*. If D merely acquires possession as a result of P's mistake, section 5 (4) is irrelevant. Thus in *Gilks* as the court held that D did not obtain ownership of the excess payment, he is guilty without recourse to section 5 (4). It was therefore useless for D to claim that there was no legal obligation upon him to return money to a bookmaker, all such contracts being void.

Theft and Deception.
It will be realised that in all cases where D obtains property from P by deception, P gives that property as a result of a mistake, *i.e.* he mistakenly believes that D is not deceiving him. Thus all cases of obtaining property by deception under section 15 (except so obtaining land) are also theft by virtue of section 5 (4). It is no excuse to state that D has become the owner of the property, as section 5 (4) allows us to regard that property as belonging to the one entitled to restoration (*i.e.* P). Students are recommended to sort out the effect of the interrelation of section 1 and section 15.

1. If D merely steals with no action from P, the charge is clearly theft.
2. Where D deceives P into temporarily parting with possession (formerly larceny by a trick) and takes the property, the better charge is under section 15, but D is also guilty under section 1, as *Lawrence* (House of Lords) declares that having the consent of the owner is no bar to a conviction.
3. If D is given the full ownership of the property and there *is deception*:
   (a) always charge section 15;

   (b) theft may be charged because of section 5 (4)—P
        made a mistake;
   (c) theft may be charged because of Lawrence (Court of
        Appeal, *obiter*).
4. If D has the full ownership of the property and there is *no
    deception*:
   (a) he cannot be guilty under section 15;
   (b) he is guilty of theft if P has a right to exclude him from
        possession (a lien);
   (c) he is guilty of theft if, receiving the money for another
        and being under an obligation to deal with it in a
        particular way, he failed so to do (section 5 (3)).
   (d) consider conspiracy to defraud if appropriate.
   (e) consider section 5 (4).

Mens Rea

   D must be proved to be dishonest, and to have had the
intention to permanently deprive. One might imagine that the
mens rea of a crime requiring appropriation would be the
intention to appropriate. If, however, D appropriates intending
to permanently deprive, he necessarily intends to appropriate.
One must therefore be careful in using *mens* and *actus* terms
here. Indeed, academic argument has placed theft as a crime of
specific intent as the accused, when he is appropriating, must
intend to permanently deprive. Thus drunkenness, though not
a defence to rape, is a defence to theft. (See Defences, *infra*.)

Dishonesty

   Though the Crown proves that D committed all the other
elements of the offence, D is not guilty if the jury do not think
he was dishonest. This element of the crime must always be
dealt with, and is usually best left until last.
   There is no definition of dishonesty, but section 2 contains a
partial one:
        "2–(1) A person's appropriation of property belonging

to another is not to be regarded as dishonest:

(a) if he appropriates the property in the belief that he has in law the right to deprive the other of it, on behalf of himself or a third person, or

(b) If he appropriates the property in the belief that he would have the other's consent . . .

(c) . . . if he appropriates the property in the belief that the person to whom the property belongs cannot be discovered by taking reasonable steps."

(2) A person's appropriation . . . may be dishonest notwithstanding that he is willing to pay for the property.

Dishonesty must be considered in two stages:

(i) Do the facts show (a), (b) or (c). If so, and the jury believe them, D is entitled to an acquittal *as a matter of law*.

(ii) If not, then the jury must simply decide whether or not they think D dishonest, and the fact that he was willing to pay will not necessarily save him.

Situations where D *is not dishonest*:

(a) *Claim of right*: D must believe he has a *legal* right to what he takes, a belief in a moral right will not do (though then D is still entitled to have the jury consider generally whether or not he is dishonest). The belief here must be honest, though presumably not necessarily reasonable.

(b) *Belief in P's consent*: D borrows coffee from a flat mate, or a small fire extinguisher to put out a fire in a nearby car. D must honestly believe that P would have consented, so that if he knows P to be unreasonably mean, he is probably not within 2–(1) (b).

(c) *Owner cannot be discovered*: D finds a coin in a crowded street and realises that it would be impossible to find the owner. Should D subsequently discover the owner and still keep the coin, his "later appropriation" will no doubt be dishonest.

Note that D only has the evidential burden of showing (a), (b) or (c), the burden of proof remains on the Crown.

What if D is not within section 2 (1)?

He may yet be acquitted if the jury believe that, as a matter of fact, he was not dishonest. Originally, the courts attempted to define dishonesty (see, *e.g. Halstead* v. *Patel* (1972)). The attempts clearly went too far. In *R.* v. *Feely* (1973) D, a betting shop manager, borrowed £30 from the till. The discrepancy was discovered as D was moved to another branch the following day. D stated that he intended to put the money back and was, at that time, owed £70 in wages by the firm. His conviction was quashed by the Court of Appeal, holding that the trial judge had been wrong to decide that D, as a matter of law, had been dishonest. Thus the question is purely for the jury. (See also *Brutus* v. *Cozens* (1973).)

Thus a defendant in Feely's position will not necessarily be acquitted; it depends on the jury. Note that the judge may withdraw the issue from the jury if there is no evidence of dishonesty—such a situation, however, is very unlikely.

There may be a problem with belief in a moral right. If D honestly believes that it is perfectly honest to take from the rich and give to the poor, can he ever be dishonest? Presumably the commonsense of juries would have to be relied on here.

Intention to Permanently Deprive

As the Act stipulates "intention," it might be supposed that recklessness as to permanent deprivation will not suffice. A look at the explanation contained in section 6 will show that this is not so:

> "6–(1) A person appropriating property belonging to another without meaning the other permanently to lose *the thing itself* is nevertheless to be regarded as having the intention of permanently depriving . . . if his intention is to *treat the thing as his own to dispose of regardless of the other's rights*; and a borrowing or lending of it may amount to so treating if . . . for a period and in circumstances making it *equivalent to an outright taking* or disposal.

(2) . . . where a person . . . parts with the property
under a condition as to its return which he may not be able
to perform, this . . . amounts to treating the property as his
own to dispose of . . ."

Where D takes P's property and later abandons it where it is
unlikely to be found, he would seem to be disposing of it
"regardless of the other's rights."

The purpose of section 6 is thus to stop D claiming he did not
possess the requisite intention where he obviously knows that P
is unlikely to get his goods back. Section 6 must *not* be pushed
too far.

In *R.* v. *Warner* (1970), D hid a workmate's tools, temporarily, out of spite. His conviction for theft was quashed by the
Court of Appeal. Though D may have "treated the property as
his own" these words are not to expand the breadth of section
1 (1). Edmund Davies L.J. stated:

"There is no statutory definition of the words 'intention of
permanently depriving'; but section 6 seeks to clarify their
meaning in certain respects. Its object is in no way to cut
down the definition of 'theft' contained in section 1 . . . its
apparent aim is to prevent specious pleas . . . But it is a
misconception to interpret it as watering down section 1."

(See also *R.* v. *Easom*, *supra*.)

Borrowing: This may amount to theft. Where D borrows P's
radio and later moves away taking it with him; there is evidence
on which a jury might find the requisite intention.

Note "The thing itself." This covers situations where D subsequently returns P's property but has extracted all its usefulness. Thus, where D takes P's monthly season ticket and uses it
on the underground until its expiry, his returning the actual
ticket then will not excuse him. What if D returns it half way
through the month, is this "equivalent to an outright taking"?

Appropriation: Note the link with section 3 (*supra*). Where
D "sells" the Coronation Coach. There is probably no appropriation, though the contrary is arguable. There would seem,

anyway, to be no intention to permanently deprive, though one might argue that D is still treating P's property "as his own to dispose of." Nevertheless, especially considering *Warner*, this would seem not to amount to an intention to permanently deprive the Crown of the Coach.

Section 6 (2) covers the situation where D pawns P's goods and, though he intends eventually to redeem them, *may* not be able to do so.

CHAPTER 7

THE THEFT ACT (2)

Abstracting Electricity

Section 13 states:

"A person who dishonestly uses without due authority, or causes to be wasted or diverted, any electricity, shall ... be liable ..."

Section 2 does not apply, so dishonesty is purely a question of fact for the jury. The section is aimed at people who "jump-lead" electricity meters, though it no doubt covers the burglar who switches on an electric light or uses the telephone. It has also been suggested that section 13 applies to the use of battery power.

It was held in *Low* v. *Blease* (1975) that electricity is not property within section 4, and thus cannot be stolen. The Act contains no special provision for gas which, presumably, is "property."

Robbery

Section 8 states:

> "(1) A person is guilty of robbery *if he steals*, and immediately *before* or *at the time* of doing so and *in order to do so*, he uses *force* on any person or *puts* or *seeks to put* any person *in fear* of being *then and there* subjected to force."

Section 8 creates *two* offences, robbery, and assault with intent to rob. As it begins "if he steals," there must always be a theft. Thus if D commits the *actus reus* of robbery, but could not be guilty of theft as he falls within section 2 (1), he is not guilty of robbery. This perpetuates the pre-Theft Act case of *R. v. Skivington* (1968), where D demanded, at knife-point, money which he believed was legally his (though quare Blackmail, *infra*).

"Force"

Force must be used on a person, thus it is not robbery for D to pull P's briefcase. It would be if D were to hit P in order to get the briefcase. Obviously, there will be borderline situations. (See, *e.g. R. v. Dawson* (1976).)

"Puts or seeks to put in fear"

This is an alternative to the actual use of force. It is not essential that P actually was afraid, as long as D intended him to be.

Note that the force or threat of force may be against "any person." Thus D is guilty if he points a gun at P's wife, telling P to hand over his money. The force, however, must be "in order to steal." Likewise, D must put a person in fear of force being used "then and there." It is thus not robbery for D to extract money from P by threatening to shoot his wife if she is miles away.

"Immediately before or at the time of stealing"

Section 8 omits the old provision of "after stealing." This

provision necessitates arbitrary line-drawing. If D hits P on the head in P's hall, in order to steal from his drawing-room, this is no doubt robbery. Where, however, he puts P in hospital in London in order to rob his country house a week later, this is presumably (though not definitely) not robbery. It is not certain how long "at the time of stealing" extends, especially if one accepts the argument that "appropriation" is a continuing act. If D is stopped, when making his get-away, at the garden gate, that seems to fall within section 8. If he is stopped some miles later and assaults his would be imprisoner, that is probably too late.

It would seem, however, that whenever there may be an appropriation, and thus an act of theft, there may be a robbery. This may include a "later appropriation." Thus if D acquires P's property innocently, and is later challenged by P with the truth, should he decide to keep it (later appropriation and thus theft) and use force to this end, he is, arguably, guilty of robbery.

Burglary

Under section 9 a person is guilty of burglary if:
>   "(1) . . . (a) he enters a building or part of a building as a trespasser and with intent to commit . . ." [theft, g.b.h., rape, unlawful damage] . . . "or
>   (b) having entered . . . as a trespasser he steals or attempts to steal anything in the building or that part of it or inflicts or attempts to inflict on any person therein any grievous bodily harm."

Thus burglary consists of trespassing and either (a) entering with intent to steal, rape, do unlawful damage or g.b.h. or, where the Crown cannot prove such intent, trespassing and committing theft or g.b.h. It is *NOT* burglary to trespass without such intent and later commit rape or criminal damage.

Trespassing

This is narrower than the tort concept. In *R. v. Collins* (1973), D decided to have intercourse (consensual or not) with P. He was about to enter through her window when she, mistaking him for her boyfriend, invited him in, and they had intercourse. D's conviction for burglary was quashed by the Court of Appeal. The decision is important as it declares;

(i) that the tort doctrine of trespass *ab initio* does not apply here;

(ii) that a trespass cannot be committed negligently here, D must be at least reckless as to the trespass;

(iii) that not only the legal owner may give consent to entry, here, of course, consent was given by the owner's daughter;

(iv) that the entry must be "substantial." D was not "substantially" inside the room when P invited him in, thus he had not trespassed. Obviously this still requires arbitrary line-drawing.

Consent is no defence if obtained by fraud. Thus if Collins had known of P's mistake, or dressed up as a gas board meter reader in order to gain entry, he would still be a trespasser.

Under the old law of burglary, D could be guilty if, though he himself did not enter, he inserted an implement with which to commit the ulterior offence. Thus D was guilty if he inserted hooks into a building and dragged out the carpet. This may arguably apply under the new law.

The doctrine of "innocent agency" may also apply. If D sends X, an adult, into a house in order to steal, he counsels burglary. If, however, X is only 9, X is incapable of committing a crime. D may still be liable, but as the principal offender, through the child's innocent agency.

Building

The definition is wider than simply houses, shops and offices, including as it does, inhabited vehicles. Wherever one attempts to draw a line though, examiners will set a question in between it.

Note "part of a building." If D is only given permission to be in one area of a building, he trespasses if he strays into another, *e.g.* a hotel guest who enters the "private" section.

As regards flats, D may enter Flat 1 though only as a means to steal in Flat 2. Presumably, he has entered a building (the block of flats) as a trespasser. The position is more difficult if, when a guest in Flat 1, he goes through Flat 2 in order to steal from Flat 3. Here the answer is unclear.

It seems that if D enters a shop intending to steal therein, he is a trespasser, as his entry is gained by fraud, *i.e.* pretence that he is a paying customer. It may also be burglary where D enters a house innocently, but later decides to steal and hides. When he comes out from his hiding place, he presumably enters another "part of a building" with the intent to steal.

Note that "steal" has its technical meaning, thus if D, *e.g.* falls within section 2 (1), he does not steal, or intend to steal, and thus is not a burglar.

Aggravated Burglary

Section 10 states:

> "(1) A person is guilty of aggravated burglary if he *commits any burglary* and *at the time* has with him any *firearms* or imitation firearms any *weapon of offence*, or any *explosive* . . . 'weapon of offence' means any article *made* or *adapted for use* for *causing injury* to or *incapacitating* a person, *or intended* by the person . . . for *such use*."

"Firearms" and "explosive" are fairly self explanatory (and see section 10 (1) (*a*, *c*). "Weapon of offence" covers three sorts of articles:

(1) those *made* for causing injury, *e.g.* coshes, knives, knuckle-dusters;

(2) those *adapted* for causing injury, *e.g.* a block of wood with nails stuck into it, a broken bottle;

(3) those *not* made or adapted for such use, *e.g.* walking sticks, pepper pots, even torches. Here the Crown must show that D *intended* to use the article as a weapon.

Weapons picked up in the house

Where D, being disturbed by P, throws P's own paperweight at him, it would seem impossible to convict, *per* section 9 (1) (*a*), *i.e.* entry with intent. It may be, however, that a conviction, *per* 9 (1) (*b*) will hold, as D does, at the time he is stealing, have with him an article which he intends to use as a weapon. It is submitted, though, that such situations are better not viewed as aggravated burglary.

N.B. Whenever a problem requires consideration of section 10, it may also require a discussion of robbery.

Handling

Section 22 (1) states:

"A person handles stolen goods if (otherwise than in the course of stealing) knowing or believing them to be stolen goods he dishonestly receives the goods or dishonestly undertakes or assists in their retention, removal, disposal or realisation by or for the benefit of another person, or arranges to do so."

According to section 24:

(i) Stolen goods includes goods stolen abroad provided such a stealing would be an offence here;

(ii) "Stolen goods" includes goods which directly or indirectly represent the stolen goods in the hands of the thief or handler;

(iii) But not if reduced into lawful possession;

(iv) "Stolen" includes goods obtained by deception or blackmail.

1. Where D sells stolen property to a "fence," both the goods and the money received are "stolen property" and if D buys goods with that money, they are "stolen goods" also. Only when the goods are passed on to a bona fide purchaser does the chain stop.

2. The goods are no longer stolen if returned to their owner, or reduced into lawful possession (usually the police). If the owner takes back his goods, or they are seized by the police, D cannot handle, or attempt to handle them. He may, however, be guilty of theft if he tries to receive them.

3. The goods must be "stolen" within section 1. Thus if the "thief" is not guilty, *e.g.* by virtue of section 2 (1), the "handler" cannot be guilty under section 22. (Though again, quare a conviction for theft if the "handler" does not fall within section 2 (1)).

4. In *Re Attorney-General's Reference* (No. 1 of 1974). a P.C. noticed items which he believed to have been stolen, in a parked car. He immobilised the vehicle and kept watch. When the owner (D) came along, he was arrested. D was charged with handling the stolen goods, the vital question being whether the P.C.'s acts had reduced the goods into lawful custody, and thus rendered them incapable of being handled. The trial judge held that they had, and this the Court of Appeal said was wrong. Their lordships stated that the jury should have been told that if they thought the P.C. was merely standing by and watching in order to ensure that the driver did not get away without interrogation, then the goods were not reduced into lawful custody. (Students should refer to *Haughton* v. *Smith* as to what that case *does* and *does not* decide).

Types of handling
   These are:
   (i) Receiving stolen goods;
   (ii) arranging to receive them;

(iii) undertaking or assisting in their retention, removal, disposal or realisation;

(iv) arranging to undertake as in (iii).

Despite this, section 22 creates only one offence.

N.B. 1. The receiving or arranging to do so need only be for the benefit of the handler, as, *e.g.* where a fence agrees to buy stolen goods. There is no requirement that D deal with the goods physically.

2. In (iii) and (iv) above, D must be shown to have performed these acts *"by or for the benefit of another person."*

"Retention" may be committed passively. In *R.* v. *Pitchley* (1972) D's son gave him money which D placed in a Post Office account. The son later told D that the money was stolen. D did nothing. He was convicted of handling and the Court of Appeal upheld the conviction. D was permitting the money to remain under his control in his account. It was also D who put the money there, so that he is not guilty purely by omission.

In *R.* v. *Brown* (1969) stolen property was placed in D's house. D did nothing in relation to it and his conviction for "assisting in the retention" was quashed by the Court of Appeal, who held that it was wrong to tell a jury that D's mere failure to inform the police necessarily amounted to so assisting.

Handling and Theft

A strict division between the two is impossible, *e.g.* any accused receiving stolen goods must necessarily commit theft. Likewise, the thief's conduct might easily include "handling" were it not for the words "otherwise than in the course of stealing." It is uncertain how long a thief is in the course of stealing, what, *e.g.* if he steals P's silver, hides it, and later arranges to collect it?

In *Stapylton* v. *O'Callaghan* (1973), D was found in possession of a stolen driving licence, with no evidence as to whether he stole or received it. The Court of Appeal held that the correct course was to convict him of theft, it being unclear whether or not he was a handler.

Mens Rea

D must know or believe that the goods are stolen.

In *R.* v. *Grainge* (1974), D's conviction under section 22 for receiving a stolen calculator was quashed as firstly, the jury may have gained the impression that the test here was objective, *i.e.* whether they thought D ought to have made enquiries, which is incorrect. Secondly, the court thought there to be "some point" in the argument that guilty knowledge must be shown to exist at the time of receipt, though this is probably only true in relation to "receiving."

It was held in *R.* v. *McCullum* (1973) not to matter that D does not know the exact nature of the property handled, provided he realises that it is stolen. Here, D was held guilty of handling guns hidden in suitcases, where D did not know what the contents were, but did know those contents were stolen.

D must also be shown to be dishonest, and section 2 does *not* apply here.

Note also the aid given to prosecution, as to the ability to raise previous convictions in evidence, given by section 27 (3).

Blackmail

Section 21 states:

"A person is guilty of blackmail if, with a view to *gain* for himself or another or with intent to cause *loss* to another he makes any *unwarranted demand with menaces* . . . unless . . . in the belief . . .

(a) that he has reasonable grounds for making the demands *and*

(b) that the use of the menaces is a proper means of reinforcing the demand."

By virtue of section 34 "gain" and "loss" refer solely to property, whether temporary or permanent, and include keeping what one has.

Thus, section 21 involves D forcing P to take action, which will result in gain to D or loss to P, by the use of "menaces."

Demand

May be by words, by conduct (pointing a revolver at P) or even by letter. In *Treacy* v. *D.P.P.* (1971) it was held that the demand was complete on D's posting of the threatening letter, thus D is guilty when he has done all in his power to bring the threat to P's attention. If *Treacy* is entirely correct (which may be doubted) the offence would be complete when D shouts down a phone to a deaf P. Surely this cannot extend to where D writes a letter to an already dead P. No question of attempt could arise here (*supra*).

Menaces

This no doubt covers threats of violence, slander of professional reputation, etc. Apart from noting that the threat must be serious, it is difficult to define "menaces" exactly. It was stated in a pre-Theft Act case:

> ". . . threats or conduct of such a nature and extent that the mind of an ordinary person of normal stability and courage might be influenced and made apprehensive so as to accede willingly to the demand would be sufficient for a jury's consideration." (*R.* v. *Clear* (1968).)

The test seems to be whether or not D uses a threat intended by him to force P out of fear or concern to act (or omit to act) in a certain way. It is irrelevant that P is prepared to ignore the threat, or is alternatively, very easily frightened unless, of course, D knows this.

"Gain" or "Loss"

As this concerns property, it is thus not blackmail to threaten P into sleeping with D, or into suicide. It is blackmail, however, to force P into lending property; there is no requirement of permanent deprivation. Nor is there a requirement that any gain actually accrues to D.

It might be thought that where D threatens P into paying a debt there is no gain or loss, as D has only got his entitlement. Nevertheless, D does receive property which he did not actually possess before his threats. The Court of Appeal in *R*. v. *Lawrence and Pomroy* (1971) appeared to have accepted that this situation may amount to blackmail, though here the debt was disputed by the victim.

"Unwarranted"

The demand is not unwarranted if D believes that he has reasonable grounds for making it, and that the use of the menaces is an appropriate way of backing it up. It is not, however, for D to prove this. He merely needs to produce evidence that this may be so, then it is up to the Crown to prove that he did not honestly believe this. Thus the more unauthordox D's moral principles, the more likely will be his story that he believed the menaces proper, though, once again, the common sense of the jury will be a factor.

In the old case of *R*. v. *Dymond* (1920) D, who was only semi-literate, wrote to a man who had made an indecent attack on her, telling him to pay up or be exposed. Though D would probably not be guilty today, the second part of the "defence" (belief that menaces were a proper means of reinforcement) would no doubt prove the more difficult test.

Where D threatens to perform an act in itself criminal, *e.g.* an assault, it is unlikely that he could believe this to be a "proper means."

N.B. Section 21 is very wide. In questions involving discussion of other offences, particularly robbery, it is worthwhile considering blackmail.

CHAPTER 8

THE THEFT ACT (3)

Discussion here is of *Theft Act* ss. 15 and 16, though students should not forget conspiracy to defraud (*supra*).

Section 15: *Obtaining Property by Deception*

"(1) A person who by any deception dishonestly obtains property belonging to another, with the intention of permanently depriving the other of it, shall on conviction . . .

(2) . . . a person is to be treated as obtaining property if he obtains ownership, possession or control of it, and 'obtain' includes obtaining for another or enabling another to obtain or retain."

Sections 4, 5 and 6 apply here, except that the proviso in section 4 relating to land does not.

Deception

Much of what is said here applies to section 16 also. The deception may be deliberate or reckless, by words or conduct and as to any fact or law, including a deception as to D's present intentions. Thus D is guilty if he takes money from P by pretending that he wishes to give it to charity.

The deception need not be by express words. It may be by conduct. In the old case of *R.* v. *Barnard* (1837) D was granted credit as the Oxford shopkeeper took his (unauthorised) wearing of the undergraduate gown to be a sign that D attended the University.

In *D.P.P.* v. *Ray* (1973), a case concerning the original section 16 (2) (*a*), there was held to be a deception when D, who had ordered a meal intending to pay for it, left after eating it and realising that he could not pay. The House of Lords held that his deception was by letting the waiter assume that he could pay after he had realised that he could not. As the waiter believed that D could pay, he did not take steps to restrain D. Note that the circumstances must be viewed as a whole. D is guilty as he makes a representation which forces P (the waiter) to act in a certain way (bring dinner). When he realises the representation is no longer true (he cannot pay) he appreciates that if P is not told, P will act to his detriment (not keep a careful eye on D). D intends to use this opportunity (*i.e.* leaving when P is not looking) to gain an advantage. Though this case is covered on its facts by the *Theft Act 1978*, it is still important as showing the breadth of "deception." Had D known from the first that he could not pay, he would have been guilty under section 15.

If D obtains goods by use of a "dud cheque" he will be liable unless he knows that, as far as can be reasonably foreseen, the cheque will be honoured on presentment (see *M.P.C.* v. *Charles, infra,* qualifying *R.* v. *Page* (1971)).

Obtaining

The deception must force P to act in a way which obtains the property. In *R.* v. *Clucas* (1949) D deceived a bookmaker into taking a bet which, had he known the truth, he would not have taken. The horse won. D's conviction for obtaining his winnings by false pretences was quashed by the Court of Criminal Appeal, as the effective cause of D's obtaining was the horse's winning of the race, not the inducement of the P to accept the bet. (On the facts, this is now an offence under section 16, though the principle remains.)

It was held in *R.* v. *Collis-Smith* (1971) that D does not "obtain by deception" where he allows petrol to be put into his tank and *then* pretends that X will pay the bill—here the property was obtained before the deception was practiced.

Belonging to Another

Section 5 (1) applies. Thus D may obtain his own property, provided P has a legal right to exclude him from it. It does not matter that D obtains ownership. (See *infra*, theft and deception.)

Mental Element

The Crown must prove (i) D's deception was *reckless or deliberate*, (ii) he *intended to permanently deprive* P, and (iii) he was *dishonest*.

(i) D is guilty if he knows or even suspects that his statement is untrue. He is not guilty if, though a reasonable man might appreciate that his statement may be false, he honestly does not. D must also intend (or at least realise) that the deception will be acted upon by P.

In *R.* v. *Greenstein* (1976) D sent applications for shares, enclosing cheques for sums of money that he did not have. D knew that he would be allocated fewer shares than he had applied for, but that his cheque would be cashed and a cheque for the balance (*i.e.* the cost of shares not allocated) sent to him. D had no authority from his bank for this temporary credit. D was found guilty under section 15, the deception being that his cheque was a valid order for which he had authority to draw. D's conviction was upheld, even on counts relating to the times when D's cheques did not "bounce," as the return cheque from the companies had arrived and been placed by D into his account. D deliberately took a chance here that his cheque might not be met, and had no authority to do so.

(ii) Section 6 applies, as necessarily modified. Where D obtains money, it is unlikely that he intends to repay those notes, so his only defence is likely to be lack of dishonesty. It is difficult to apply section 6 completely to deception cases. How, *e.g.* can D part with property under a condition which he may be unable to fulfil, by deception?

(iii) Section 2 does *NOT* apply. In *R.* v. *Potger* (1970) D deceived P into ordering magazines, though there was no question that the magazines were not worth their price. D's conviction was upheld by the Court of Appeal, who turned to certain pre-Theft Act cases in order to provide help in defining dishonesty. This, however, was before *Feely* (*supra*) and it would now seem that dishonesty is a question of fact for the jury alone.

It is probably safe to ensure that a "claim of right" might indicate that D is not dishonest.

Section 16 Obtaining a Pecuniary Advantage by Deception

D, dishonestly, obtains a pecuniary advantage for himself or another, by deceiving P. "Pecuniary advantage" is not a wide term like "dishonesty" but its ambit is specifically prescribed by section 16 (2), (*b*) and (*c*). Any "pecuniary advantage" must thus be proved to come within one of the following.

Section 16 (2) (a): The original (2) (*a*) has been replaced by the *Theft Act 1978*, removing the sub-section that caused considerable trouble.

Section 16 (2) (b): Covers the case where D borrows money by overdraft, takes out an insurance or annuity contract or obtains better terms on such a contract, by deception.

Normally, D's obtaining a loan by deception will entail his receiving money, but it may simply increase his borrowing rights. He also obtains an overdraft by deception if he deceives X into taking a cheque backed by a cheque card (without informing X that he has not the authority to do so) which necessarily requires P (his bank) to meet the cheque. This was the case in *M.P.C.* v. *Charles* (*infra*).

The rest of this sub-section covers the situation when D, *e.g.* falsely tells a Life Insurance Company that he has had no illnesses, or omits to tell a motor insurance company of a string of convictions for bad driving, thus incurring a much lower premium than if he had been truthful.

Section 16 (2) (c): Covers two situations not criminal under the old law.

(i) D is given the opportunity to earn remuneration or greater remuneration in an office or employment, by deception. D, falsely, tells P that he is a graduate, as a result of which P employs him. D is not guilty under section 15 as it is his work that obtains the salary (*R.* v. *Lewis*). He is guilty under section 16. He is also guilty if, *e.g.* he states that he has a better degree than he does have, thus securing a higher salary.

(ii) He is given the opportunity to win money by betting. Thus *Clucas* would commit an offence under section 16, though not under section 15.

Mental Element
1. There is no requirement of permanent deprivation.
2. Dishonesty is required, see *supra*, section 15.

Theft Act 1978

As already stated, this Act replaces section 16 (2) (*a*) of the 1968 Act. It creates the following three offences:
(i) obtaining services from another by deception:
(ii) evading liability by deception:
(iii) making off without payment.
Section 1 states:

"(1) A person who by any deception dishonestly obtains services from another shall be guilty of an offence. (2) It is an obtaining of services where the other is induced to confer a benefit by doing some act, or causing or permitting some act to be done on the understanding that the benefit has been or will be paid for."

Section 1 thus refers to the obtaining, by deception, of services which are provided for reward. It would thus catch the defendant who books into P's hotel, pretending that his employer will pay. (See *R.* v. *Nordeng* (1976) under the old section 16 (2) (*a*).)

It has been held in relation to section 16 (2) (*b*), to be irrelevant that the pecuniary advantage is obtained from a person other than the one deceived. In *M.P.C.* v. *Charles* (1976) the defendant secured the right to gamble by pretending to a casino manager that he had authority from his bank to make out several cheques, covered by his cheque card. The bank was obliged to meet the cheques, and thus D's overdraft was obtained by deception. It was no good for D to show that, though he deceived the casino, the advantage was obtained from the bank. It would seem that, under section 1, the person deceived must be the provider of the services.

Section 2 states:

"(1) . . . where a person by any deception:

(a) dishonestly secures the remission of the whole or part of any existing liability to make a payment whether his own liability or another's; or

(b) with intent to make permanent default in whole or in part of any existing liability to make a payment . . . dishonestly induces the creditor . . . to wait for payment . . . or forego payment; or

(c) dishonestly obtains any exemption from or abatement of liability to make a payment;

shall be guilty of an offence.

(2) . . . 'liability' means legally enforceable liability . . .

(3) [in] (1) (b) a person induced to take in payment a cheque . . . is to be treated . . . as being induced to wait for payment."

This section applies to a defendant who dishonestly obtains credit by not paying, or repaying, money. Under (*a*), D deceives P into allowing him not to pay all or part of a debt, *e.g.* D tells P that he has lost his job (falsely) and P releases him from a debt.

Under section 1, D may secure a temporary respite, but in section 2 it must be proved that D intended to default permanently, thus the debtor who gives a dud cheque simply to gain a few days grace is not covered.

Obtaining an exemption of liability to make payment under para. (*c*) would cover the defendant who pretends to be a pensioner, this gaining free access to a theatre.

Section 3 states:

"(1) . . . a person who, knowing that payment on the spot for any goods or service is required or expected from

    him, dishonestly makes off without having paid . . . with
    intent to avoid payment . . .
  (3) Subsection (1) above shall not apply where the supply of
the goods or the doing of the service is contrary to law, or where
the service done is such that payment is not legally enforceable."

Section 3 covers defendants such as Ray, without the need to
discover any specious deception. It may be that problems will
be encountered with the civil law, as, *e.g.* where D has been
given an unsatisfactory meal and storms out of a restaurant
without paying. It is thought that rather than concentrate on
possible civil law complications, the courts may hold such conduct to constitute an *actus reus*, and concentrate the jury's
attention on the question of dishonesty.

Chapter 9

DEFENCES

Strictly, a defence applies where D admits committing the *actus*
with the necessary *mens rea*, but adduces a reason to show why
he is not criminally liable. The term is sometimes applied,
however, to situations where D denies, because of a "defence,"
that he actually formed the *mens rea* at all.

1. Infancy

If D is below *10* years old, there is an irrebuttable presumption
that he is incapable of committing a crime, even though he may
actually have committed an *actus reus* intentionally. If an adult
abets a child in committing a "crime," the adult may be liable as
principal via the doctrine of "innocent agency."

If D is between *10 and 14*, he will only be guilty if the crown prove a "mischievous discretion." This was held in *R*. v. *Gorrie* (1919) to entail proof of D's knowing that his act was "gravely, seriously wrong."

There is an irrebuttable presumption that a child under 14 cannot commit rape, though he can, if between 10 and 14 and possessing a mischievous discretion, be convicted of indecent assault.

2. Self-Defence and Protection of Property

Under *Criminal Law Act 1967*, s. 3, a person may use reasonable force to prevent crime or effect an arrest. This no doubt applies to crimes against his own person or property, and offenders who have injured him or stolen or damaged his property.

There were previously doubts about the use of force in the protection of one's family or friends, but these seem resolved by *R*. v. *Palmer* (1971) where it was also held to be impossible to lay down a formula for self-defence, but made clear that one employing force in such a situation can hardly be expected to "weigh to a nicety the exact measure of his necessary defensive action."

3. Insanity

As a successful plea here invariably results in long-term incarceration in "hospitals" like Broadmoor, it is seldom raised, a mentally disturbed defendant being more likely to plead Diminished Responsibility on a murder charge. There are three times at which insanity may be established:

(a) Before the accused is brought to trial

The Home Secretary on the advice of two medical practitioners may commit D to hospital under the *1884 Criminal Lunatics Act*, if he believes it not practicable to bring D to trial.

(b) Before the trial commences

Here D is found "unfit to plead" under the *Criminal Procedure (Insanity) Act 1964*. D must be proved incapable of understanding the trial, pleading, giving evidence, etc., by reason of insanity.

It was held in *R.* v. *Padola* (1960) that where D had forgotten the events in question because of "hysterical amnesia" he was still fit to plead.

The law here was criticised, as, though D must plead unfitness before the trial's start, he might have gone on to be acquitted. This is partly remedied by section 4 of the 1964 Act, which gives the judge a discretion to postpone the question of unfitness until the end of the prosecution's case, thus allowing D to claim that there is no case to answer.

Unfitness is tried by a separate jury. Thus if they find D fit to plead, a separate jury tries the substantive case. If raised by D, the burden is upon him on the balance of probabilities, if by the Crown, upon them to prove beyond all reasonable doubt.

(c) At the trial

Here the issue is "was D insane when he committed the act?" The law is governed by the *McNaghten Rules* of 1843. These are advice from the judges of the Queen's Bench at to when an insanity plea might be accepted. The party claiming insanity must show:

> "that at the time of committing the act, the party accused was labouring under such a defect of reason, from disease of the mind, as not to know the nature and quality of the act he was doing, or, if he did know it, that he did not know he was doing what was wrong."

Thus:

   (i) D had a *disease of the mind,*
   (ii) which results in a *defect of reason* so that:
      (a) *he did not know what he was doing or*
      (b) he did not know that *what he was doing was wrong.*

(1) "Disease of the mind"

This is a *legal*, not a medical, test, though medical evidence will obviously be relevant.

In *R.* v. *Kemp* (1956) D hit his wife, causing g.b.h. He was found to be suffering from arteriosclerosis, which caused a blood clot in D's brain, resulting in a lack of consciousness. D claimed he was an automaton. Devlin J. held that the question of insanity must be left to the jury, holding it to be irrelevant whether the defect is caused by degeneration of the brain or any other form of mental derangement. His lordship goes on:

> "In my judgment the condition of the brain is irrelevant and so is the question whether the disease is curable or incurable or whether it is temporary or permanent."

In *R.* v. *Quick* (1973) D claimed that his committing an assault was due to hypoglycaemia, D being a diabetic. It was held at first instance that, even though this condition resulted from the use of insulin, D was only entitled to plead insanity and not automatism. The Court of Appeal reversed this, stating:

> "A malfunctioning of the mind of transitory effect caused by the application ... of some external factor such as violence, drugs, including anaesthetics, alcohol and hypnotic influences cannot fairly be said to be due to disease" (*per* Lawton L.J.).

(2) "Defect of reason"

This is more than depression, resulting in absentmindedness (*R.* v. *Clarke* (1972)). It must result in *either* (a) or (b).

(a) D did not know what he was doing, *i.e.* did not appreciate the "nature and quality of his act." It is not enough for D to show an "irresistible impulse" (though quare a plea of Diminished Responsibility). If D's dillusions make him think facts to be otherwise than they are, the court will look at them as if true. Thus if D believes P to be a Martian about to destabalise him and D kills P, D will have a defence of insanity. If, however, his insanity leads him to believe that P is sleeping with his daughter, and he sets out to kill P, he cannot plead insanity as, had the facts been as D believed them, they would have afforded no defence.

(b) D did not believe his actions to be wrong, which means contrary to the laws of the land. In *R.* v. *Windle* (1952), D, who was almost certainly insane, killed his wife, afterwards stating "I suppose they'll hang me for this." The trial judge held that there was no question of insanity to go before the jury. The Court of Appeal held this to be correct. Though there was probably evidence that D had a disease of the mind, there remained the issue of D's responsibility. If, as was obviously the case, he knew that he had broken the law, he could not plead insanity.

N.B. 1. If D wishes to plead insanity he must prove it, on the balance of probabilities. This seems unobjectionable except as to (2) (*a*), where D does not know what he was doing and thus has no *mens rea*.
2. The verdict is "not guilty by reason of insanity" (by virtue of section 1 of the 1964 Act).
3. By the *Criminal Appeal Act 1968*, section 12, it is possible for D to appeal against a finding of insanity, regardless of who raised the issue at the trial.

4. Mistake

N.B. Mistake is important in *two* ways:
1. D claims that because of his mistake, he did not have the relevant *mens rea* for the crime;
2. D admits both the actus and the mens, but denies liability because of his mistake.

1. The leading case is *Morgan* v. *D.P.P.* (1975), D invited two colleagues to have intercourse with his wife. They claimed that they honestly, though unreasonably, believed her to have consented. Though they were not believed, the House of Lords made it clear that had this been true, they would not be guilty of

rape. The mistake thus need not be reasonable. This is because rape is intercourse without consent, and the *mens rea* is intended intercourse, and intending (or being reckless) that it be without consent. If D believes P consents, he is no rapist. All *Morgan* does therefore is make it clear that negligence will not do as to the mens rea of rape, the issue of reasonableness going only to the issue of proof as to whether D actually did believe what he claims.

Likewise in theft, D must intend to take the property of another. If he honestly, albeit unreasonably, believes the property to be his, he is not guilty.

2. Here D, *e.g.* assaults P intentionally, but claims mistake as a defence, *e.g.* he mistakenly believed that P was about to kill him. It is uncertain whether or not this mistake has to be reasonable as well as honest. D is not denying the mens rea of assault, so *Morgan* is not directly in point. Note The House of Lords refused to remove the requirement of reasonableness from the bigamy cases (see *R.* v. *Tolson*, 1889), and also refused to consider cases of strict liability. This position is confusing. In bigamy, if the *mens rea* is the intention to marry while being married, an honest, though unreasonable belief that one's spouse is dead is a denial of *mens rea*. Thus the ratio in *Morgan* logically overrules *Tolson* as far as the latter requires reasonableness. Only if one views the *mens rea* of bigamy as requiring simply the intention to marry (see Lord Fraser) is an honest mistake a plea of mistake as a defence rather than lack of mens. It seems that statutory offences (*i.e.* of strict liability or negligence), are to be treated as exceptions to the principles in (1) and (2) above.

5. Drunkenness

1. This includes, for these purposes, a state of mind induced by drugs.

2. If the drunkenness takes the form of a recognisable mental disease, *e.g.* Delirium Tremens, D is treated as if the insanity rules apply.

3. Should D decide to perform a criminal act, and take drink in order to give himself "dutch courage," his drunkenness will not excuse him. (*A.G. for N. Ireland* v. *Gallagher* (1963)). (Though, technically, one might argue that the *mens* and *actus* do not coincide in time.)

4. Should D's drinking not deprive him of his senses, but simply make him more prone to criminal tendencies, it is no defence (*R.* v. *McCarthy*, *supra*).

5. Where the drink (or drugs) does effectively deprive D of his reason, he has a defence *only to a crime of "specific intent."* This will usually entail conviction for a lesser offence, *e.g.* manslaughter on a charge of murder.

Thus in *D.P.P.* v. *Beard* (1920) D was held guilty of murder when, hopelessly drunk, he killed a girl during a rape attempt. Lord Birkenhead L.C. makes it clear that only in crimes of specific intent will drunkenness be a defence.

(*N.B.* murder, before 1957, could be established by proof that D intended and committed a felony, here Rape. Thus the Crown need only prove intent to rape, and rape is not a crime of specific intent.) See also *Gallagher* (*supra*).

This rule appears logical, until one examines "specific intent." Murder requires this, rape does not. One head of murder is "intent to kill." One *can* (it seems) be too drunk to form the intent to kill. It is not enough to argue that a crime of specific intent requires intention, whereas other crimes may be committed recklessly as murder (see *Hyam*) may be committed recklessly.

What does this tell us about "specific intent"?

The Courts in cases like *Beard* were generous. The then rules of evidence allowed them to say that D must have intended the natural results of his action. (Though thought *not* to be the law from *D.P.P.* v. *Smith*, it was certainly the law in 1920). For the courts to allow D, even though only as regards certain crimes, to plead that he did not intend to kill, etc., *was* generous. After 1967 (s. 8,6*C.J.A.*) the position should be different. D must be proved to have *mens rea* for any crime. If he was too drunk to form *mens rea*, he cannot be guilty, regardless of whether the crime is one of so-called "specific intent." This was argued in *R.* v. *Lipman* (1969) though was, somewhat unconvincingly, rejected by Lord Widgery C.J.

In *D.P.P.* v. *Majewski* (1976), D, who was drunk, assaulted a police officer. He was convicted of assault occasioning a.b.h. He appealed contending that because of section 8, the Crown had to prove that he had the mens rea for the assault, which pointing to his drunken state, he claimed he had not. This was rejected, eventually by the House of Lords.

Lord Elwyn Jones L.C. argues that section 8 refers to "relevant evidence," and for a crime not requiring specific intent, evidence of drunkenness is irrelevant.

More pragmatic is Lord Edmund Davies. His lordship admits the illogicality of the rule, but declares that it must necessarily remain the law. (A victory for common sense over logic.) Quare where D's drunkenness renders him so stupified as to be an "automaton?"

6. Where D's drunkenness is involuntary, as where his drink is "laced," he has a defence to crimes of "basic intent" also.

6. Duress

Traditionally, this applies where D is threatened with immediate death or physical violence into commission of a crime. The threat must obviously be a grave one, and D must, effectively, have no other choice than to commit the act.

In *R.* v. *Hudson* (1971) D committed perjury. This was because she had been threatened by X, who watched from the gallery as she gave evidence. Her conviction was quashed by the Court of Appeal, Lord Widgery C.J. accepting that it is unrealistic to expect a defendant to rely on police protection, which can obviously not protect her always. Thus "immediate threat" may be interpreted loosely.

Duress applies to most crimes, though quare treasonable activities (Lord Goddard C.J. in *Steane* evidently did not accept that duress was a defence here, which might explain that case) and *murder*.

In *Lynch* v. *D.P.P. for N. Ireland* (1975), D was forced into abetting members of the I.R.A. who committed murder. The House of Lords held that duress *might* afford a defence here, and should have been left to the jury. (At his retrial, D was convicted despite duress having been considered by the jury).

Duress is not a defence, and thus cannot be considered by a jury, on a charge of murder as principal. In *Abbot* v. *The Queen* (1976), D was ordered by X, of whom he was terrified, to help in hitting P and burying her alive. His conviction for murder was upheld by the Privy Council:

> "If duress affords a defence . . . to all murderers who are principals in the second degree, . . . sometimes . . . murderers in this class will be lucky in that Lynch's case will allow them to go free. This does not . . . afford any sound reason for changing the law by ruling that duress should allow the man who does the actual killing to go free." (Lord Salmon).

Both cases were majority decisions. Quare whether Abbott was a "principal in the first degree" or not?

7. Necessity

Again, D feels forced to commit a crime. There is little authority on this defence. It might be argued that where a statutory offence requires an action to be performed "unlawfully," D will not be guilty where his action is necessary, *e.g.* moving P's car because it is near a bomb (see *R.* v. *Bourne* (1939)).

Otherwise the defence hardly exists. It clearly does not apply to murder (*R.* v. *Dudley and Stevens* (1884)), and in both *Buckoke* v. *G.L.C.* (1971) and *Southwark* v. *Williams* (1971) its narrowness was stressed. It may probably only be pleaded where there is a situation of imminent death or serious injury to someone.

Index

Accessory, 15
Accomplice, 15
Actual Bodily Harm
  assault occasioning, 49
Actus Reus, 2–5
  attempt, of, 23
  causation, 5–7
  conspiracy, of, 21, 27
  drunkenness affecting, 4
  homicide, of, 33
  mens rea, non-coincidence of, 12
  omission, by, 7
  theft, of, 52
Aiding and Abetting, 15–20
  counselling, 16, 17
  crime, after, 16
  joint enterprise, 17
  principal, acquittal of, 18
Animal,
  theft of, 59
Appropriation, 53
  consent, and, 54
  force, by, 56
  sale, by, 57
Assault, 46 *et seq.*
  a.b.h., occasioning, 49
  aggravated, 48
  consent to, 48
  g.b.h., occasioning, 49
  intent to rob, with, 69
  transferred malice, by, 49
  words alone, 47
Assistant Offender, 19
Attempt, 22–27
  actus reus of, 23
  equivocal acts, 24
  impossible acts, 25
  mens rea of, 22
  proximate acts, 23, 25
  strict liability, offence of, 22, 23
  theft, 54

Battery, 47
Blackmail, 52, 76–78
  demand, 77

Blackmail (*cont.*)
  menaces, 77
  unwarranted demand, 78
Burden of Proof, 2
Burglary, 52, 70
  aggravated, 72, 73
  building, from, 71

Causation, 5–7
Child,
  10 to 14 years, 86
  10 years, under, 85
Common Assault, 1, 47
Conspiracy, 26–30
  actus reus, of, 27
  common law, 26
  corrupt public morals, to, 29
  crime of strict liability, to commit,
    28
  defraud, to, 27, 29, 59, 79
  impossible, to do, 21, 31
  parties to, 30, 31
  statutory, 26, 28, 32
  "Wheel," 27

Deception, 63, 79
  evading liability by, 83
  making off without payment, 83
  mens rea of, 64
  mental element in, 81
  obtaining by, 80, 83
  pecuniary advantage, obtaining
    by, 82, 83
Diminished Responsibility, 40, 41
Dishonesty, 64–66
  claim of right and, 65
  consent and, 65
Drunkenness, 90–92
  provocation and, 39
  specific intent, and, 91
Duress, 92, 93

Electricity, abstracting, 68

Firearms,
  burglary, for use in, 72

Grievous Bodily Harm, 35, 36, 50
  assault and, 49
  burglary, and, 70
Gross Negligence, 43

Handling Stolen Goods, 58, 73–76
  mens rea of, 76
  receiving, 75
Homicide, 32 *et seq.*

Incitement, 20, 21
  attempt, 21
  impossible crime, 21
Indictment, 2
Infancy, 85
Infanticide, 45
Innocent Agency, 18, 21, 71, 85
Insanity, 40, 86
  arteriosclerosis, 88
  defect of reason, 88
  hysterical amnesia, 87
  unfitness to plead, 87
Intent,
  conditional, 54
  specific, 10
Intention, 3, 8
  murder, in, 35
  permanently deprive, to, 66–68
  recklessness and, 36

Jury, Provocation to be Left. 16, 39, 41

Liability,
  strict, 13, 14
  vicarious, 14, 17
Lien, 60

Manslaughter, 37–44
  constructive, 41
  gross negligence, due to, 43
  involuntary, 41–44
  suicide pact, under, 46
  unlawful omission, by, 42
  voluntary, 37–41
McNaghten Rules, 40, 87
Mens Rea, 3, 8–12
  abettor, of, 18, 19

Mens Rea (cont.)
  actus reus, non-coincidence of, 12
  attempt, of, 22
  deception, of, 64
  g.b.h., of, 50
  handling, of, 76
  mistake, 89
  murder, of, 33–36
  strict liability and, 15
  transferred malice and, 12
Mistake, 89
Motive, 3
Murder, 33–36
  mens rea of, 33–36
  specific intent, 11, 34

Negligence, 9
Necessity, 93, 94
Noxious Thing, 51

Plants, 59
Poaching, 61
Poison, 51
Property, 58
  another, held for, 61
  belonging to another, 60
  deception, obtaining by, 63
  mistake, obtained by, 63
Provocation, 37
  drunkenness and, 39
  jury, to be left to, 39

Rape,
  burglary, and, 70
  child under 14, 86
  consent, mistaken, 90
  specific intent, not crime of, 11
Recklessness, 9
  objective, 10
  surgeon, by, 9
Robbery, 52, 69

Self-Defence, 86
Specific Intent, 91
Strict Liability, 13
Suicide, 45
Summary Offence, 2
  incitement to commit, 20

Theft, 52 *et seq*.
  actus reus of, 52
  burglary, and, 70
  mistake, due to, 61, 62
  part-owner, by, 60
  petrol station, at, 54
  plant, of, 59
  transfer of ownership, on, 55
  trick, by, 54

Theft (*cont.*)
  trustee, by, 59
Transferred Malice, 11
  assault and, 49
Trespass, 71

Vicarious Liability, 14

Wounding, 49